Richbaub's Introduction to Middle School Grammar

A Foundation in Grammar for Middle School Writers

by Richard M. Gieson, Jr.

Third Edition

© 2023

Second Edition Published in 2018
First Edition Published in 2012

Richbaub's Ink Works

Cover Image Credit: © Corbis - Fotolia.com

Introduction

Teaching grammar is important, but not many agree on how to best deliver this knowledge to our students or how deep to go. A complicating factor is that conveying this special knowledge about the language does not immediately yield sublime prose with every written draft or perfect elocution with each utterance, but what can be counted on is that, in whatever academic or professional pursuits lie ahead for our students, an understanding of grammar must be in place if they are to have a chance to become expert communicators via the English language.

On the most-practical level, teaching writing in middle school is certainly facilitated when teachers and students are familiar with action and linking verbs and can identify introductory elements like prepositional and participial phrases, subordinate clauses, and adverbs. Understanding grammatical forms also brings clarity to punctuation rules.

In high school, when communicating about writing, teachers frequently use grammatical terms with students, such as fragment, subordinate clause, misplaced modifier, preposition, conjunction, pronoun usage, run-on, parallel structure, agreement, etc., and a background in grammar undoubtedly makes this knowledge more accessible.

But how much time can middle school teachers allot to teaching grammar when they are also charged with teaching other aspects of writing, as well as reading, literature, and vocabulary? Which grammar topics should be covered and in what sequence? Which topics do not require formal study? Which topics should be left for future study?

Good news: *Richbaub's Introduction to Middle School Grammar* was created to answer these questions for middle school teachers!

Richbaub's Introduction to Middle School Grammar is suitable in scale, rich in spiraled content, and developmentally appropriate for students. Building on the basic grammar taught at the elementary level, Richbaub's completes students' foundation in rudimentary grammar and secures a context for all future references to and lessons in grammatical things.

In addition, Richbaub's very clearly communicates to students that the study of grammar is all about better writing, i.e., understanding the English language's patterns and components and practicing putting words together in the clearest, most effective, and most correct way.

And for teachers, Richbaub's is the grammar strand you've been looking for as it fits seamlessly beside the reading, literature, writing, and vocabulary study in today's middle school English classrooms.

Welcome to Richbaub's!

Richard Gieson, Jr.

Table of Contents

Chapter 1

Prepositions & Prepositional Phrases

Prepositions and prepositional phrases are everywhere! Knowing about them will help you immensely when analyzing the parts of a sentence. A good understanding of prepositional phrases will also help advance your writing skills because there are comma and pronoun usage rules associated with prepositional phrases. In addition, a familiarity with prepositions helps with properly capitalizing titles, and advanced writing concepts like agreement, sentence variety, and parallel structure are easier to understand when you know about prepositional phrases. Are you ready? Let's go!

Introduction to Prepositions & Prepositional Phrases

A. **Prepositions** are words that <u>begin little phrases</u> that describe something or someone's location in space or time (*in* the cupboard, *with* Janie, *above* the house, *after* the movie). These little phrases are called **prepositional phrases**.

B. You will need to memorize a list of prepositions.

C. Here is a list of 40 of the most commonly used prepositions:

about	below	in	out
above	beneath	in front of	over
across	beside	inside	through
after	between	instead of	to
against	beyond	into	toward
along	by	near	under
around	down	next to	until
at	during	of	up
before	for	off	with
behind	from	on	without

D. The best strategies for memorizing the prepositions:

1. **Break It Up** – Try memorizing in stages by learning ten (one column) at a time. Once you can recite the first column's prepositions in order, memorize the second column. Then recite both columns in order, etc.

2. **Learn by Letter Groups** – Work to remember how many prepositions begin with the letter "a." As you can see, there are eight "a" prepositions. Number your paper 1-8 and work on writing down the eight "a" prepositions in order. Once you've mastered the eight "a" prepositions, follow the same strategy for the eight "b" prepositions, the two "d" prepositions, the two "f" prepositions, and so on.

3. **Make Up a Story** – Break your story up into four parts, one for each column of the prepositions above. Try to fill your story with details that are easy to picture in your mind. For example, begin the first column by imagining this scene: _About_ noon _above_ the rocky cliffs _across_ the foamy river, hungry hawks chased _after_ rabbits scurrying _below_ the... Memorize one column of your story at a time until you know the whole story. **Not feeling up to creating your own story? Check out "Prepositions in Verse" on p. 168 where you'll find a complete story you can use to help you memorize the prepositions!**

4. **The Airplane Trick** – This technique is not quite as orderly as the others, but it can really help when you are wondering if a word is a preposition or when you get stuck and are trying to remember prepositions you may have forgotten. What you do is picture a bird flying around an airplane—an airplane cruising with its windows open. Now, where can the bird be in relation to the plane? _Inside_ the plane, _above_ the plane, _behind_ it, _in front of_ it, _over_ it, _under_ it, etc. Get it? This technique doesn't work for all of the prepositions on the list above, but you may be able to come up with prepositions that aren't on the list that your teacher will be kind enough to give you credit for, like _upon_, _underneath_, etc. Good luck!

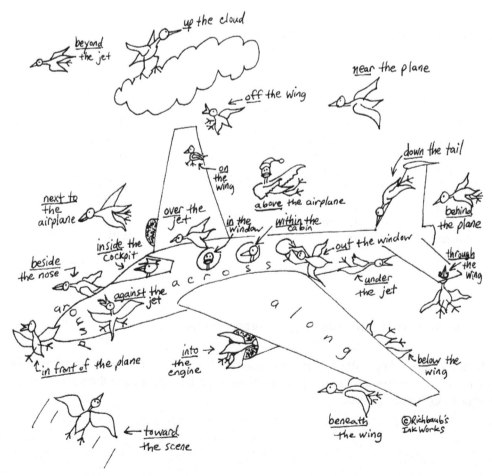

Practice for Evaluation 1

Memorize the prepositions from the first column on p. 9. When you feel like you're ready, write them below. The first letter of each one has been provided for you.

Now study the prepositions from the second column. When you feel like you're ready, write them below from memory. The first letter of each one has been provided for you.

a_____

b_____

a_____

b_____

a_____

b_____

a_____

b_____

a_____

b_____

a_____

b_____

a_____

d_____

a_____

d_____

b_____

f_____

b_____

f_____

Continue by studying the prepositions from the third column. When you feel like you're ready, write them below. The first letter of each one has been provided for you.

Finally, memorize the prepositions from the fourth column. When you feel like you're ready, write them below. The first letter of each one has been provided for you.

i_____

i_____

i_____

i_____

i_____

n_____

n_____

o_____

o_____

o_____

o_____

o_____

t_____

t_____

t_____

u_____

u_____

u_____

w_____

w_____

➤ **Evaluation 1: Memorizing Prepositions** – Are you ready now?

The Basic Structure of a Prepositional Phrase

A. A prepositional phrase begins with a preposition and ends with a noun or pronoun.

B. In between the preposition and the noun or pronoun, there may be one or more descriptive words (adjectives and/or adverbs).

C. Examples:

preposition → at home ← noun

preposition → in the car ← noun
(descriptive word ↓)

preposition → between the chairs ← noun
(descriptive word ↓)

> Yes, *the* is a descriptive word! All of the articles (*a*, *an*, & *the*) are officially categorized as adjectives. Not the most descriptive buggers, but adjectives nonetheless. More about adjectives later…

preposition → near her ← pronoun

preposition → on the long, wooden dock ← noun
(descriptive words ↙ ↓ ↘)

preposition → before the game ← noun
(descriptive word ↓)

preposition → from the very large container ← noun
(descriptive words ↙ ↓ ↘)

preposition → after everyone ← pronoun

 **Exercise 1**

Write your own prepositional phrases. Use prepositions that begin with the given letters.

1. a _____   4. f _____

2. b _____   5. w _____

3. i _____   6. t _____

Bonus Info!!

Some people will tell you never to end a sentence with a preposition. The reason for this rule is that a preposition should begin a prepositional phrase, and if you have a preposition at the end of a sentence, either there is no phrase or the phrase has been broken apart somehow.

For example, compare the following sentences:

> A. Where is the magazine at?

> B. Where is the magazine?

Clearly, the preposition *at* in sentence A is completely unnecessary. Therefore, sentence B would be considered more correct.

Now compare the following sentences:

> A. Whom did you give the book to?

> B. To whom did you give the book?

Sentence B would be considered more grammatically correct because the prepositional phrase "to whom" is intact. (In case you're wondering, *whom* is used instead of *who* because you must use *whom* in prep. phrases, not *who*.)

However, there are times when it's ok to end a sentence with a preposition. A line attributed to former British Prime Minister Winston Churchill shows how awkward a strict adherence to this rule can be:

Never ending a sentence with a preposition is a rule up with which I will not put!

(The sentence sounds much better if you *break apart* the prepositional phrase "with which." Try it!)

Study of the Objects of Prepositions

What is an Object of a Preposition, and where is it?

A. The last word in a prepositional phrase (the noun or pronoun that completes the phrase) is called the "object of the preposition," or "o.p." for short.

B. In the examples below, the objects of the prepositions are: *home, car, chairs, her, dock, game, container,* and *everyone*.

C. Here are a few more examples of prepositional phrases with their parts labeled inside sentences:

descriptive words   descriptive word
prep.   o.p.   prep.   o.p.

(After the big game) the boys (on the team) ate ice cream sandwiches.

descriptive word
prep.   o.p.

The horse (behind the fence) bit my sister's hand!

D. Sometimes a word from the prepositions list appears in a sentence, but it is NOT functioning as a preposition. You can tell because it has no object (o.p.).

Compare the following sentences. Both use the word *before*, which is on your list of prepositions. However, in only one of the sentences is *before* functioning as a preposition.

 A. I had a cup of water before bedtime.

 B. Elijah had never seen a bridge so high before.

Above, in sentence B the word *before* is NOT a preposition—it has no object and is therefore <u>not</u> beginning a prepositional phrase. In sentence B *before* is an adverb.

In sentence A, "before bedtime" is a prepositional phrase, and so *before* <u>is</u> functioning as a preposition in sentence A.

E. Here's another example:

 A. Jayda went inside after the ballgame.

 B. The puppy walked inside the doghouse.

In sentence A, "inside after the ballgame" is NOT a prepositional phrase. "After the ballgame" is a prepositional phrase, and *inside* is all by itself, functioning as an adverb in this sentence.

In sentence B, "inside the doghouse" IS a prepositional phrase.

F. Remember how a prepositional phrase is built: It begins with a preposition and ends with a noun or pronoun, and it may also have a descriptive word or two between the preposition and o.p.

"Inside the doghouse" fits this pattern, but "inside after the ballgame" does not fit this pattern because the word *after* is not a descriptive word—it begins its own prepositional phrase, "after the ballgame."

Exercise 2

Part 1: Write prepositional phrases and circle the objects of the prepositions (o.p.'s). Use prepositions that begin with the given letters.

1. t _____

2. a _____

3. f _____

Part 2: In each of the following sentences, put parentheses around each prepositional phrase you see, and circle the objects of the prepositions. One sentence does not have a prepositional phrase.

4. The boy at the carnival won three huge stuffed animals.

5. Beneath my bed is a dust bunny village.

6. Mary crossed the river near the old bridge.

7. My black cat has never gone outside before.

8. With a grin my dad tore the wrapping from his birthday presents.

9. At midnight the owl always begins his nightly hooting.

10. Paper is recycled at the factory.

Humor Break!

My three favorite things are eating my family and not using commas!

Multiple Objects of Prepositions & Conjunctions

A. Once in a while, you will see a prepositional phrase that has two or three objects (o.p.'s).

For example:

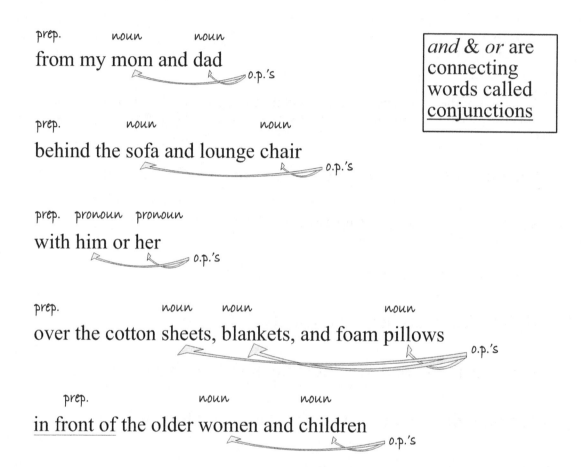

and & or are connecting words called <u>conjunctions</u>

B. When a prepositional phrase has more than one object, we say it has a <u>compound object</u>.

Here are some prepositional phrases with compound objects:

after the game and picnic

in the drawers and cabinets

with Aubrey, Ryker, or Jake

Exercise 3

Part 1: Write prepositional phrases that have more than one object of the preposition (o.p.). Use prepositions that begin with the given letters.

1. a _____

2. b _____

3. u _____

4. w _____

5. i _____

6. o _____

Part 2: In each of the following sentences, put parentheses around the prepositional phrases, and circle the o.p.'s. Most of the sentences have more than one prepositional phrase, and some prepositional phrases have compound objects of the preposition.

7. Everybody at the zoo brought money for lunch and souvenirs.

8. Animals on land and sea are hunted by humans.

9. With pencil and paper in hand, I headed to the art room.

10. You can build almost anything with a hammer, nails, and wood.

11. On Monday or Tuesday I will help Tim with his homework.

12. Is your birthday in the summer or in the winter?

13. For tests and quizzes I study with flashcards.

Extra Practice for Evaluation 2

<u>Part 1</u>: Surround prepositional phrases with parentheses. One sentence does not have any prepositional phrases.

1. Joe went to the game at the stadium.

2. The boy is running around and screaming.

3. Does anyone care about this TV show?

4. After dinner and the concert Vince and Alina seemed quite exhausted.

5. The dogs and cats bark and meow during the nighttime.

<u>Part 2</u>: Write prepositional phrases that have <u>one</u> object of the preposition, and circle each object. Use prepositions that begin with the given letters.

6. b _____

7. f _____

<u>Part 3</u>: Write prepositional phrases that have <u>more than one</u> object of the preposition (compound o.p.), and circle each object. Use prepositions that begin with the given letters.

8. i _____

9. n _____

<u>Part 4</u>: Write sentences that contain <u>two</u> prepositional phrases, and surround each phrase with parentheses.

10. _____

11. _____

<u>Part 5</u>: Write a sentence that has at least one prepositional phrase which includes <u>two</u> objects of the preposition. <u>Surround each phrase with parentheses.</u>

12. _____

_____

 Evaluation 2: Composing Prepositional Phrases – Are you ready now?

Chapter 2

Nouns & Pronouns

Armed with a sound knowledge of nouns and pronouns, you will be more skilled at telling where a prepositional phrase ends as well as better able to identify subjects in a sentence, which is something coming up in Chapter 5.

Advanced writing concepts are also linked to an understanding of nouns and pronouns, things like when to use I vs. when instead to use me, *how subject-verb and pronoun-antecedent agreement work, and how using concrete nouns can improve the details and imagery in your writing.*

Study of Nouns

All prepositional phrases end with either a noun or a pronoun, so this is a good time to review nouns and pronouns.

A. Nouns are the most basic part of speech in the universe. Nouns are the words we use for the people, places, things, and ideas all around us, words like *boat, freedom, Africa, fork, grass, pencil,* etc.

B. The nouns that we always capitalize, like the names of people and countries, are called **Proper Nouns**. All other nouns are considered **Common Nouns**.

C. The nouns that describe things you experience with one of your five senses (feel, hear, smell, taste, and see) are called **Concrete Nouns**. For example, *paper, car, breeze, aroma, flower,* and *thunder* are all concrete nouns.

D. Nouns that describe things you cannot experience with one of your five senses, things like *liberty, fairness, sin, hope,* etc., are called **Abstract Nouns**.

E. And be sure to recognize that nouns can be proper and concrete at the same time, or abstract and common at the same time, etc.

Humor Break!

"An abstract noun," the teacher said, "is something you can think of, but you can't touch it. Can you give me an example of one?"
"Sure," a teenage boy replied. "My father's new car."

Exercise 4

Part 1: Using prepositions that begin with the given letters, write prepositional phrases that have…

proper nouns for objects of the preposition (o.p.'s).

1. u _____

2. i _____

3. b _____

common nouns for o.p.'s.

4. a _____

5. o _____

6. n _____

concrete nouns for o.p.'s.

7. i _____

8. o _____

9. f _____

abstract nouns for o.p.'s.

10. w _____

11. d _____

12. t _____

Part 2: Surround prepositional phrases with parentheses. One sentence does not have any prepositional phrases.

13. In Oregon it can be quite rainy along the coast.

14. Everyone from the city and suburbs should vacation in the countryside during the summer months.

15. I have never seen a wild boar outside.

16. Andrew ran over the hill near the grocery store on his way to school.

17. The cat rubbed my leg beneath the table at dinnertime.

18. The ball shot through the hole in the fence.

Study of Pronouns

A. Pronouns are a close cousin to nouns. Pronouns are alternate words we use for people, places, things, and ideas. For instance, in place of the nouns *Joe* and *Mary*, you might instead simply use the pronoun *they*. Instead of saying the noun *box*, you could use the pronoun *it*.

B. As you can see, although pronouns are used for the same kinds of things as nouns (people, places, things, and ideas), pronouns are not as specific as nouns.

C. One reason pronouns exist, however, is to provide us some variety.

D. Here's what a world without pronouns might sound like:

> *"Bob and Mabel were married after Bob got out of the Navy. Bob flew Navy jets. Bob was 18 when Bob met Mabel, but Bob didn't have the courage to ask Mabel to marry Bob until Bob turned 25, so Bob and Mabel dated for over seven years before Bob and Mabel got married."*

With pronouns you can refer to someone named Bob as *he* or *him* or someone named Mabel as *she* or *her* once in a while instead of saying their specific names all of the time. Isn't that just wonderful?

Pro-noun Rally

E. Pronouns simplify your life, too.

For example, let's say you were named Jimbo, and you and seven friends went out to a movie. The next day your dad returns from a long business trip, and you and your dad are eating breakfast together. In a world without pronouns, the conversation might go something like this:

Dad: *"Ah, good to be back home."*

Jimbo: *"Yeah, nice to have Dad back, too, Dad."*

Dad: *"So, Jimbo, what has Jimbo been up to?"*

Jimbo: *"Last night Bob, Tyler, Nick, Mike, Kevin, Doug, Curly, and Jimbo went to the movies."*

Dad: *"Did Jimbo and Jimbo's friends like the movie?"*

Jimbo: *"Yeah, Bob, Tyler, Nick, Mike, Kevin, Doug, Curly, and Jimbo loved the movie."*

Dad: *"Did Jimbo or Jimbo's friends get any popcorn?"*

Jimbo: *"Nah. Neither Jimbo nor Bob, Tyler, Nick, Mike, Kevin, Doug, or Curly had any money left over."*

Instead of naming all of the people you're talking about, you can simply say *everyone*, or *they*, or *we*. Isn't that a nice thing?

Do you see the need for pronouns?

F. The toughest thing to know about pronouns is all the different types of pronouns. We're going to concern ourselves with Personal Pronouns first.

Personal Pronoun Usage in Prepositional Phrases

A. Personal Pronouns are by far the most-used pronouns, as well as the most widely mis-used! There are two main types of personal pronouns. One kind can NEVER be used in a prepositional phrase.

Objective Case Personal Pronouns	Nominative Case Personal Pronouns
me	I
you	you
her	she
it	it
him	he
us	we
them	they
whom	who

Fyi, the nominative case is sometimes called the <u>subjective</u> case.

As you can see, *you* and *it* are both objective <u>and</u> nominative case personal pronouns. They are "all-purpose" personal pronouns.

B. What's most important here is that when using Personal Pronouns as objects of Prepositions (o.p.'s), you MUST choose a word on the <u>Objective</u> Case Personal Pronouns list. Get it? OBJECTive case for OBJECTs of the preposition?

C. In other words, the words *I, she, he, we, they,* and *who* can NEVER be used in prepositional phrases!!

Examples:

> **CORRECT:** John went fishing (with me and my dad).
> *"with my dad and I" would be <u>in</u>correct*

> **INCORRECT:** (To my mom and I), chocolate is a wonderful thing.
> *"To me and my mom" would be correct*

> **INCORRECT:** They sat (near Bill and I).
> *"near me and Bill" would be correct*

> **CORRECT:** This magazine article is (about him and us).
> *"about he and we" would be <u>in</u>correct*

D. Here are some things to know that can help you remember which personal pronouns are objective case and which ones are nominative case:

Objective Case Pronouns – **O**K for o.p.'s	**N**ominative Case Pronouns – **N**EVER use for o.p.'s
Most have an "m."	None contain an "m."
Only *me* ends in "e."	Several end with "e."
Acronym: Notice that the last letters can spell out "Mr. Tummes."	Acronym: Arranged as below, the last letters spell out "Tie Eye" followed by a picture of a tie (the "U" in *you*) and a picture of an eye (the "O" in *who*).

```
        TW                           T
  HH   YHH                     SH    YW
  IE   IOEOMU            I  H  HEW   OH
  MR   TUMMES            TIE  EYE    UO
```

E. Below, fill in the Objective and Nominative Case Personal Pronouns yourself:

Objective Case – **O**K for Prepositional Phrases

Personal Pronoun List:

he
her
it
you
them
us
she
they
him
we
whom
who
me
I

M R   T U M M E S
_____

Nominative Case – **N**EVER use in Prepositional Phrases*

T I E   E Y E   U O

*Of course, it's ok to use *you* and *it* in prepositional phrases.

Exercise 5

You will need to use Personal Pronouns for this exercise:

Personal Pronoun Refresher Box	
Objective Case Personal Pronouns	**Nominative Case Personal Pronouns**
me	I
you	you
her	she
it	it
him	he
us	we
them	they
whom	who
As you can see, *you* and *it* are both objective <u>and</u> nominative case personal pronouns. They are "all-purpose" personal pronouns that can be used anywhere!	

<u>Part 1</u>: Write prepositional phrases that…

have a personal pronoun for each object of the preposition (o.p.).

1. a _____

2. t _____

3. i _____

each have <u>two</u> personal pronoun o.p.'s.

4. n _____

5. b _____

6. w _____

<u>Part 2</u>: Circle only the <u>correct</u> prepositional phrases:

7. between you and I

8. for Jim and me

9. for me and them

10. to me

11. from you and her

12. to who

13. beneath whom

14. with she

15. with her

16. to her and I

Part 1: Write prepositional phrases using a different personal pronoun for each o.p. Also, use prepositions that begin with the given letters.

1. t _____   3. u _____

2. a _____   4. b _____

Part 2: Write prepositional phrases with <u>compound</u> objects (see p. 18). <u>Use only personal pronouns</u> for the objects of the prepositions. Also, use prepositions that begin with the given letters.

5. i _____

6. f _____

7. o _____

Part 3: Editing for improper prepositional phrase construction. Put parentheses around each prepositional phrase, and correct any that use personal pronouns incorrectly.

8.   Last weekend there was an intense ping pong match between

9. my dad and I. Before the first game we made a big pitcher of iced

10. tea and set it on a stool next to the table.

11.   "You serve first," said my dad. I smashed a curving serve to

12. him. He flinched but recovered in time and returned it well.

13. "You're getting pretty good with that serve, son," said my dad.

14.   Just then, my twin sisters came into the room. "For who is

15. this tea? Is it for Mary and I?" said my sister Sue.

16.   "No—it's for Dad and me," I shouted between hits.

17.   "Why is he always so mean to us, Dad?" Mary asked.

18.   "He's wrapped up in this game with I," said my dad.

19.   Just then a ball sailed toward her. Mary ducked. The ball

20.   ricocheted off the wall and plopped right into the tea pitcher. Sue

21.   looked at Mary. Mary looked at Sue. Dad looked at me. "Fine," I

22.   said. "Let's give some tea to she and Sue."

23.   "Yuck!" they said. "We don't like ping pong tea!"

Humor Break!

A zookeeper wanted to get some extra animals for his zoo, so he decided to compose a letter. The only problem was that he didn't know the plural of *mongoose*. He started the letter: "To whom it may concern, I need two mongeese."

No, that won't work. He tried again: "To whom it may concern, I need two mongooses." Is that right?

Finally, he got an idea: "To whom it may concern, I need a mongoose, and while you're at it, send me another one."

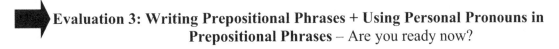
Evaluation 3: Writing Prepositional Phrases + Using Personal Pronouns in Prepositional Phrases – Are you ready now?

BTW: There will be a Personal Pronoun Refresher Box on the test.

Indefinite, Demonstrative, & Reflexive Pronouns

A. Indefinite Pronouns – They're called "indefinite" because it's not definite who, what, or how many people or things you're talking about when you use them.

B. *Everyone*, *nothing*, and *somebody* are all indefinite pronouns. In fact, <u>all of the words ending in "one," "thing," and "body" are indefinite pronouns</u>.

Agreement, a topic you'll study when you're older, involves rules with indefinite pronouns...

C. Other indefinite pronouns include:

few	neither	many	none
several	any	some	much
both	all	most	one
either	other	more	no one

Which one?
Which one?
Either.
How much?
Some.
You're SO indefinite!
Any many most?
Aargh!

©Richbaub's Ink Works

D. For your information, indefinite pronouns can sometimes switch to being adjectives (a kind of descriptive word):

In the following sentence, *some* is the object of a preposition and a pronoun:

(To <u>some</u>), boxing is a barbaric sport.

This next sentence also includes *some*, but it describes the word *people* and is therefore a descriptive word (adjective) and not a pronoun.

Boxing is the greatest sport in the world (to <u>some</u> people).

In the following sentence, *all* is the object of a preposition and a pronoun:

The Constitution promises life, liberty, and the pursuit of happiness (for <u>all</u>).

Below, *all* describes the word *insects* and is therefore a descriptive word (adjective), not a pronoun.

My mom is terribly frightened (by <u>all</u> insects).

☆ Do you see how <u>the part of speech of a word depends on how it is used?</u> ☆

E. **Demonstrative Pronouns** – The pronouns used when you point to something: *this, that, these,* and *those.* These words can also be adjectives, depending on how they're used.

For example:

In the following sentence, *these* is the object of a preposition—it's not a descriptive word; it's a pronoun being used in place of the names of all of the things being referred to:

I want you to make room (for these).

In the sentence below, *these* describes something, so it's functioning as an adjective:

Yesterday I ate a box (of these cookies) for dessert.

F. **Reflexive Pronouns** – Words ending in "self" and "selves" are reflexive pronouns: *myself, yourself, himself, ourselves, themselves,* etc.

A reflexive pronoun reflects on his reflection.
© Richbaub's Ink Works

Exercise 6

Part 1: Using prepositions that begin with the letters provided, write prepositional phrases that have…

indefinite pronouns for o.p.'s. (Be sure they're not being used as adjectives!)

1. a _____

2. t _____

3. u _____

reflexive pronouns for o.p.'s.

4. i _____

5. w _____

6. b _____

demonstrative pronouns for o.p.'s. (Be sure they're not being used as adjectives!)

7. a _____

8. f _____

9. n _____

personal pronouns for o.p.'s.

10. o _____

11. b _____

12. i _____

> ***Have you noticed yet that the personal pronoun *her* can sometimes act as an adjective? If you use *her*, put it at the <u>end</u> of your prepositional phrase to make sure it is a pronoun.

Part 2: Write sentences of <u>at least ten words</u> that include…

13. a reflexive pronoun.

_____

14. a demonstrative pronoun. (Be sure your pronoun is not being used as an adjective!)

_____

15. an indefinite pronoun. (Be sure your pronoun is not being used as an adjective!)

_____

Extra Practice for Evaluation 4

<u>Part 1</u>: Using a different preposition for each, write prepositional phrases that have <u>compound</u> o.p.'s.

use demonstrative pronouns for both o.p.'s:

1. _____

use personal pronouns for both o.p.'s:

2. _____

use indefinite pronouns for both o.p.'s:

3. _____

use reflexive pronouns for both o.p.'s:

4. _____

<u>Part 2</u>: Write one prepositional phrase where the word *that* is used as an o.p. and one prepositional phrase where the word *that* is a descriptive word (adjective).

that as an o.p.:

5. _____

that as a descriptive word (adjective):

6. _____

<u>Part 3</u>: Recalling the pronoun types

7. Write out the personal pronouns you are allowed to use in prepositional phrases (hint – Mr. Tummes):	8. Write eight indefinite pronouns:
9. Write five reflexive pronouns:	10. Write out the four demonstrative pronouns:

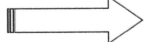

There's More

Part 4: Put parentheses around each prepositional phrase, and correct any that use personal pronouns incorrectly.

11.   In a quiet backyard in the town of Chester, three boys played a

12. game of kickball. Mike was up first. "Roll a nice, slow one to me," he

13. called out to the pitcher.

14.   "If you kick one to Dennis or I, you're a dead duck!" said Richie, who

15. was pitching. Richie turned and whispered to Dennis, "Move over to the left.

16. We'll nail him if he goes for second base." Dennis was moving over when,

17. at that moment, Mike stroked a ball between Richie and he. Dennis

18. chased it to the fence. "Throw it to me!" yelled Richie.

19.   Mike rounded first base and wondered to himself if he could beat

20. Dennis's throw to second base. Mike's eyes widened as Dennis released a

21. laser through the hot summer air toward him, Richie, and second base, but

22. it was rising, and the ball whizzed completely over the heads of Richie and

23. he. Mike raced for third base.

24.   "If Richie and I lose," thought Dennis, "I'll be really upset with

25. myself." Racing for the loose ball, Richie grabbed it, whirled, and, falling

26. away, whipped it at Mike. Thwack!

27.   "I'll get you for this, Richie," said Mike as he examined the welt

28. developing on his leg, for his furious race around the bases had

29. suddenly ended just inches from home plate!

➡ **Evaluation 4: Using Pronouns in Prepositional Phrases** – Are you ready now?

BTW: There will be a Personal Pronoun Refresher Box on the test.

Study of Comma Usage with Prepositional Phrases

A. When beginning a sentence with one or more prepositional phrases, people often have an urge to use a comma afterward. However, there is no strict grammar rule about this.

Using commas after introductory prepositional phrases (prep. phrases at the beginning of sentences) is actually <u>optional</u>.

"I hate commas in the wrong places."
- *Walt Whitman, famous American poet*

B. Good writers know, though, that using commas unnecessarily is bad form. So, **after one introductory prepositional phrase, you should mostly** <u>**avoid**</u> **using a comma:**

Compare the following sentences:

> At school I look forward to recess the most.

> At school, I look forward to recess the most.

Above, the comma in the second sentence is <u>not</u> necessary and should therefore be omitted.

C. **Once in a while, you need to use a comma after a single introductory prepositional phrase in order to avoid confusion.**

Compare the following sentences:

> To some French dressing on a salad adds zest to any meal.

> To some, French dressing on a salad adds zest to any meal.

The comma definitely helps—without the pause you might think the sentence is about either how only some French people like dressing on their salads or even how some French folks enjoy getting dressed on top of a salad!

D. Also, there are certain prepositional phrases typically used at the beginning of a sentence that REALLY make you feel like inserting a comma after them. **After phrases like "for example," "in other words," "in conclusion," "by the way," etc., it's ok to use a comma.**

E. After <u>more than one</u> introductory prepositional phrase, commas are more acceptable but still optional:

Compare the following sentences:

In the corner of my bedroom I saw a large cockroach climbing the wall.

In the corner of my bedroom, I saw a large cockroach climbing the wall.

The comma in the second sentence is acceptable since there are two consecutive prepositional phrases beginning the sentence, but is it really necessary?

F. The bottom line? **After prepositional phrases at the beginning of sentences, if you can do without a comma, don't use one.**

Never throw commas around whenever and wherever you want for no good reason. A "gut feeling" is not a good enough reason!

(Other comma rules are more strict, like those regarding compound sentences or items in a series, etc. Do you know some of these comma rules?)

Ultimately, good writers use a comma <u>only when their gut feeling lines up with a grammatical rule</u>; otherwise, commas are to be avoided.

Extra Practice for Evaluation 5

Part 1: Write sentences of 8-12 words that begin with one or two prepositional phrases. Pay close attention to comma usage. Surround each prepositional phrase with parentheses.

1. _____

_____

2. _____

_____

3. _____

_____

4. _____

_____

Part 2: Locating Prepositional Phrases in sentences and identifying Objects of Prepositions

Surround each prepositional phrase with parentheses, AND circle each object of the preposition.	Is the o.p. a noun (N) or a pronoun (PRO)?
5. The meal provided enough food for everyone.	
6. Two eagles were soaring high in the sky above.	
7. The clothes on display were very colorful.	
8. The squirrel scurried up the giant redwood tree.	
9. A tornado circled the town just after midnight.	
10. For many, Irish stew is a hearty meal. *(Do you know why there is a comma after this introductory prep. phrase?)*	

 Evaluation 5: Nouns vs. Pronouns + Comma Usage with Introductory Prepositional Phrases – Are you ready now?

Chapter 3

Verbs

Many times, the key to improving a sentence lies in improving the sentence's verb. A better verb can improve a sentence's clarity as well as its imagery, and paying attention to the placement of verbs plays a role in having better sentence variety.

Therefore, a grammatical understanding of verbs is a very powerful thing to possess—it's one of the advantages expert writers have over average writers. Experts' verb knowledge includes knowing the difference between action and linking verbs, understanding helping verbs, and being able to discern the difference between active and passive voice writing. If you pay close attention, you too can possess this special knowledge!

A. In dealing with verbs, it's impossible to avoid mentioning subjects, too.

Do you know what a subject is? A subject is simply the main person or thing a sentence is about. Subjects are always nouns or pronouns.

However, before getting in depth about subjects, it's important to first get in depth about verbs.

Introduction to Verbs

B. Every sentence has at least one verb. There are two kinds of verbs: action verbs and linking verbs.

C. <u>Action Verbs</u> ⚙

Sometimes the verb tells what the subject of a sentence does, did, or will be doing. This is when the verb is showing <u>action</u>. Verbs showing action have been cleverly named Action Verbs.

> **In the afternoon Bill *built* a bookcase for his son.** (The subject, Bill, did something—he *built* a bookcase.)

D. Action verbs don't just show physical action like building, running, and shoving. They also show mental or emotional activity. The following sentences all have action verbs:

1. Alex *loves* his dog.
2. Kate *thought* about her project for two weeks.
3. For his birthday Will *wanted* a new bicycle.

E. Linking Verbs ∞

Sometimes, a subject of a sentence isn't really doing anything; instead, it is just *being* something. In this case, the verb is called a Linking Verb because it is the word that <u>links</u> the subject to something it is or is being.

> **After the game I *was* very happy.** (*I* is the subject and *happy* is what the subject was being—these words are linked by the verb *was*.)

> **That notebook *is* really thick.** (*Notebook* is the subject and *thick* is what it is—these words are linked by the verb *is*.)

F. Compare Action and Linking verbs with the examples below:

<u>Action Verb</u>:

Rashid *brought* the cake to the party. (*Brought* is a verb showing action—the subject, Rashid, is actually doing something.)

<u>Linking Verb</u>:

Zoe *was* upset yesterday. (*Was* is a linking verb—the subject, Zoe, is not doing anything; there is no action. Zoe is just being *upset*.)

G. One of the most important things someone can learn regarding grammar is how to tell the difference between action verbs and linking verbs. More on that later.

H. For now, let's concern ourselves with trying to recognize which word in a sentence is the verb.

Humor Break!

Substitute teacher: Are you chewing gum?

Billy: No, I'm Billy Anderson.

How to Find the Verb in a Sentence

A.   Here's a little trick you can use to narrow your search for a sentence's verb: Make the sentence say the opposite of what's actually being said.

Example sentence: **In the morning Michael brushed his teeth.**

B.   <u>Step 1</u>: Insert a word or words that make the sentence say the "opposite":

did not brush
In the morning Michael ~~brushed~~ his teeth.

C.   <u>Step 2</u>: Now go back to the original example sentence and scour <u>the general vicinity</u> where you had to make the change. This is where the verb will be found.

D.   In our example the word *brushed* is the verb.

E.   Other examples:

You read that entire book last night?

did not read
You ~~read~~ that entire book last night?

 Since this is where we had to make the change to make the sentence say the opposite, we know the verb is somewhere in this area. (*Read* is the verb in this sentence.)

The baseball hat was on the shelf behind the counter.

was not
The baseball hat ~~was~~ on the shelf behind the counter.

 Since this is where we had to make the change to make the sentence say the opposite, we know the verb is somewhere in this area. (*Was* is the verb in this sentence.)

Exercise 7

Part 1: Underline the verb in each sentence. **In one sentence, two words go together to make the verb.** In the other sentences, the verb is a single word.

> **Hint:** Verbs are NEVER inside prepositional phrases, so patient, wise students will first mark prep. phrases to make searching for verbs easier!

1. On Tuesday we drove through the Painted Desert in Arizona.

2. The kids over there were on my track team last spring.

3. The lady behind the counter glared at me and my friend.

4. No one enjoys soggy cereal.

5. I have noticed three tiny eggs in the nest on that branch.

 Did you find the two-word verb? Verbs that include more than one word are called "verb phrases," which you will soon learn more about...

Part 2: Once you have correctly identified the verbs in the sentences above, list them below, then take a stab at deciding if each is action (A) or linking (L).

Verbs from the sentences above:	Circle A or L:
1. _____	A or L ?
2. _____	A or L ?
3. _____	A or L ?
4. _____	A or L ?
5. _____	A or L ?

Hang in there—much more is to come about how to tell the difference between action and linking verbs!

A Big Reason Verbs Can Be So Difficult to Master

A. Every sentence has at least one verb, but as you're beginning to see, verbs can look and work differently from sentence to sentence.

B. Since verbs are such shape shifters, there are many terms associated with the study of verbs. So far you have been introduced to three terms:

Action Verbs   Linking Verbs   Verb Phrases

C. Of these terms, students have the most trouble grasping exactly what a **verb phrase** is.

D. Before getting in depth with action verbs and linking verbs, and before we learn even more terms related to verbs, let's develop some familiarity with what exactly a "verb phrase" is.

E. In the simplest terms, verb phrases are verbs that include more than one word. Verbs do not always consist of more than one word, but often they do; that's just how the sometimes confusing English language works. Sorry!

Examples:

sentence	verb
I will be staying at a cabin near Lake Woodsong.	will be staying *(verb phrase)*
Surprisingly, your puppy sat quietly between us.	sat *(NOT a verb phrase)*
Colorful t-shirts are my favorite ones.	are *(NOT a verb phrase)*
He has become a very good friend.	has become *(verb phrase)*
We should hurry.	should hurry *(verb phrase)*

F. Can you see that <u>**verb phrases** are simply verbs that include more than one word?</u>

The extra words in these verbs (*will, be, has, should*) are called "helping verbs."

More about helping verbs coming soon to a page near you!

Verb Phrases vs. Single-Word Verbs

Below, the trucks help you visualize verb phrases, which include "helpers"; the cars represent single-word verbs, which have no helpers.

Tomorrow we  to the gift shop.

My brother  to college last week.

No one at the party  the banana cupcakes.

She  over the hot coals!

That TV show  my dad's favorite.

> If you're paying close attention, you will notice that some verbs, like *is*, work alone sometimes while other times they are part of a verb phrase.

Henry  incorrect about the date.

Humor Break!

A man is washing his car with his son. The son asks, "Dad, can't you just use a sponge?"

Verbs in the Infinitive Form

A. When verbs are first "born," they are in a form called the "infinitive form." The infinitive form of a verb looks a lot like a prepositional phrase—but it's NOT a prepositional phrase!

B. Here's a verb in the infinitive form: **to cook**. Here's another: **to sing**. So the infinitive form is *to* + a verb.

C. Of course, *to* can also be a preposition, but *to* + a verb is NOT a prepositional phrase–there there are no verbs in prepositional phrases.

D. Below, circle only the prepositional phrases:

to me	to eat	to be	to wonder
to walk	to the store	to Joseph	to begin

Do you understand the difference between infinitives and prepositional phrases that begin with *to*?

E. With a verb in its infinitive form, you can't make a sentence by just adding a subject, i.e., you can't say, "Mary to cook." Of course, you can say, "Mary cooks."

The verbs that have subjects—the ones you need to make a sentence—are <u>never</u> in the infinitive form.

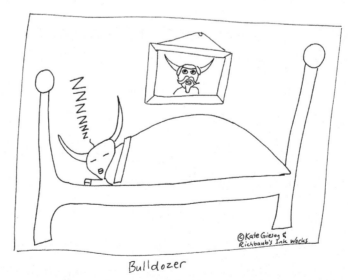

Bulldozer

F. Think of an infinitive as an egg. To use the verb, you crack it open and get something completely new and usable.

G. You *can* use verbs in the infinitive form in your sentences. Just remember that an infinitive is never THE verb—the one that goes with the subject. In other words, a verb in the infinitive form is never the thing the subject is being or doing.

Examples:

I | like | to go (to the movies) (on Saturdays).

Above, *I* is the subject and *like* is the verb. "To go" is an infinitive. You see, the subject isn't <u>going</u> anywhere; the subject <u>likes</u> something.

Josephine always | wanted | to be (in a movie) (with a Hollywood star).

Above, *Josephine* is the subject and *wanted* is the verb. "To be" is an infinitive. Josephine was not <u>being</u> anything; she <u>wanted</u> something.

More Verb Forms

A. Verbs have many different forms. The infinitive form is just one form. Two other forms are the present tense and the past tense.

Here is an example of one verb's various forms:

infinitive	present tense		past tense	
to ask	base form	**ask:** "I ask," "We ask," etc.	"ed" form	**asked:** "I asked," "You asked," etc.
	"s" form	**asks:** "She asks," "He asks," etc.		
	"ing" form	**asking:** "I <u>am</u> asking," etc.		

⬆

FAQ's:

B. What's the word *am* doing in there right above the arrow??

The word *am* is <u>helping</u> the verb work in this sentence. You couldn't say, "I asking."

Actually, *am* has even become part of the verb. The verb in this sentence would be "am asking."

Other words we use to help verbs work are *was, be, were, can, may,* and many more! For example:

<u>was</u> asked   <u>were</u> asking   <u>can</u> ask   <u>may be</u> asking

C. What about the future tense??

To speak about doing something in the future, English requires you to use one or more <u>helping verbs</u>. For example:

She **<u>will</u> ask** you about your homework. *(The verb in this sentence is "will ask.")*

My brother **<u>will be</u> asking** you for a ride to school. *(The verb in this sentence is "will be asking.")*

Study of Helping & Main Verbs in Verb Phrases

A. Sometimes a verb is made up of a few words in order to get the verb into just the right tense or to express just the right meaning:

Jenna <u>jogs</u> in the park. (The verb is a single word.)

Jenna <u>is jogging</u> in the park. (The verb is made up of two words.)

Jenna <u>should have been jogging</u> in the park. (The verb is made up of four words!)

B. Again, multiple-word verbs are called "verb phrases," so a sentence may contain a single-word verb OR a verb phrase.

C. In a verb phrase the last word is the "main verb." The other words are "helping verbs."

Under the bridge Johnny <u>may be fishing</u> for trout.

helping verbs = may, be
main verb = fishing
verb = may be fishing

D. It's important to really understand that in a verb phrase, the last word is always the "main verb"; the other words are "helping verbs," and **the whole thing together is what you would call "the verb."** So, if you're looking at a sentence that has a verb phrase and your teacher asks, "What's the verb in this sentence?" don't just state the *main* verb—*state the entire verb phrase*.

E. **Words ALWAYS used as <u>just</u> helping verbs:**

would	can	may
could	will	might
should		must

Factoid

These words weren't always confined to just these forms; their other forms have more or less simply fallen out of usage. English is an ever-evolving language!

"Retired" forms of...

- *will*: wilt, wouldst

- *could*: canst, couldst

- *should*: shall, shalt, shouldst

- *may*: mayest, mayst

F. The following words are used sometimes as helping verbs and sometimes as main verbs—and some can even be used as single-word verbs. You might think of these guys as "all-purpose" verbs:

be	are	is	have	do
been	am	was	had	does
		were	has	did

G. Examples:

He **is** in the kitchen. (*Is* is single-word verb in this sentence.)

He **is swimming** in the ocean. (Here, *is* is now a helping verb. *Swimming* is the main verb. What we would call "the verb" is "is swimming.")

I **have been** to Maine in the summertime. (*Been* is often a helping verb, but in this sentence it is the main verb of a verb phrase. *Have* is a helping verb. The verb is "have been.")

H. Consider the following sentence:

The team with the star quarterback should have won that game.

Now, if your teacher were to ask you, "What is the verb in this sentence?" of course you would answer

_____ .

(Did you answer correctly?)

I. CHALLENGE: Turn and talk to a neighbor and explain what a helping verb is! (HINT: See item "A" on p. 47.)

Exercise 8

Part 1: Circle the pronouns (see p. 25 & 30-31 if you need a refresher on pronouns). <u>You may circle one or more than one word in each line</u>.

1.	Tim	I	many	all	road	some
2.	we	group	this	team	mom	us
3.	walk	to	been	anyone	several	people

Part 2: Circle the personal pronouns below that you are allowed to use in a prepositional phrase (see p. 25 if you need a refresher on personal pronoun rules for prep. phrases). <u>You may circle one or more than one word in each line</u>.

4.	he	whom	him	I	she
5.	you	they	her	we	it
6.	me	us	who	them	him

Part 3: In the line below each sentence, write out one part of the sentence as directed.

7. The military men met with the president to plan a strategy for the war.

   What's the <u>infinitive</u> (see p. 44) in the above sentence? _____

8. At the end of the game the star player should have made that layup.

   What's the <u>verb</u> in the above sentence? _____

9. Thomas has never sat between Jennifer and me before.

   What's the <u>prepositional phrase</u> in the above sentence? _____

10. That missed field goal would have given my team the lead.

   Write only the <u>helping verb(s)</u> from the above sentence: _____

11. I pointed to the chili powder and told my sister never to cook with that.

   What's the <u>demonstrative pronoun</u> (see p. 31) in the above sentence? _____

12. John was being very rude during David's presentation yesterday.

   Write only the <u>main verb</u> from the above sentence: _____

Incredible Verb Search

Verbs to find:

was walking
did run
slammed
am seeing
should leave
will be
could have been
ate
jog
must go
throw
have read
become
had
scrape
might push
would be driving

```
N U Z W H D O D L D L Z H H G
L Q E O N A N T I J J C S E N
L Q M U A X V D H V P U S M I
E B L L I W R E Z R P J L O K
D A H D E U R L R T O P A C L
L V E B N V O C H E E W M E A
J Q V E W S A G M O A Y M B W
X Y N D G S I E T N A D E L S
O C D R Q M G H L S Y N D F A
A L K I T H J S U D U I U U W
U Z F V S C R A P E L M R U C
U M W I M X T U Z U C U W J T
T A I N A M S E E I N G O A Z
H T N G J L Q M R W N G P H J
N E E B E V A H D L U O C C S
```

Are you paying attention to the fact that verbs are sometimes made up of one word and sometimes made up of more than one word?

How to Find the Verb Phrase in a Sentence

A. Verbs are fairly easy to find in a sentence, but with verb phrases, it can be difficult to properly identify the <u>complete</u> verb phrase.

Here's an example:

Teacher: "Tammy, what's the verb in the following sentence?"

The boy has been fishing from the dock for three hours.

Tammy: "That's easy! The verb is *fishing*!"

Teacher: "Wrong! Looks like you're going to need to come to that three-hour extra help session this weekend."

Tammy: (weeping) "Really?"

Teacher: "Yes, really. The verb is 'has been fishing.'"

B. In order to avoid the fate awaiting Tammy, you need to be very careful when looking for the verb in a sentence.

THE VERB IS FISHING.

C. Do you remember the little trick you can use to narrow your search for a sentence's verb?: *Make the sentence say the opposite of what's actually being said.*

Example sentence:

On Monday I stayed at school for extra help in math.

D. Step 1: Insert a word or words that make the sentence say "the opposite":

had not
On Monday I ~~stayed~~ at school for extra help in math.
ʌ

E. Step 2: Now go back to the original example sentence and scour the general vicinity where you had to make the change. This is where the verb and all of its parts (if it's a verb phrase) will be found.

F. In our example, the word *stayed* is the verb, a single-word verb.

G. Since you now know about verb phrases, please scour <u>the area</u> where you make a change in the sentence—<u>the verb may include more than one word</u>:

do not
I love my new pet snake. (*Love* is the verb in this sentence.)
ʌ

not
The boy in the back row has been sleeping during class. ("Has been sleeping" is the verb in this sentence.)
ʌ

not
Our delayed chartered flight will leave for Atlanta in three hours. ("Will leave" is the verb in this sentence.)
ʌ

NOTE: *Please do not mistake infinitives (to + verb) for verb phrases! (See page 44 if you forget what an infinitive is.) Even though infinitives are technically verbs and are made up of more than one word, they are NOT verb phrases! For example, there is <u>no</u> verb phrase in the following sentence:*

The boy wanted to eat in the restaurant at the top of the mountain.

(The verb is *wanted*.)

 **Exercise 9**

In this exercise helping verbs play an important role:

Helping Verbs				
would could should will can	may might must	*are *am *be *been *is *was *were	*have *had *has	*do *does *did
*Multi-purpose word. Can be a helping verb, a main verb in a verb phrase, and/or even a verb all by itself.				

Part 1: Underline the verbs. If the verb is a verb phrase, include ALL of the words (helping verb[s] **and** main verb). Consider marking prepositional phrases to make your search easier.

1. The children did sit at their desks.

2. Around the edge of the lake the geese searched for a snack.

3. The cookies inside the box have melted in the summer heat.

Part 2: In the sentences below, surround the prepositional phrases with parentheses. A verb can never be inside a prepositional phrase, so be careful.

4. My grandfather lives with mom and me in our log cabin.

5. The grass next to the fence was growing very tall.

6. Those jets may fly in the air show on Saturday.

Part3: Go back to sentences 4, 5, & 6 above and underline the verbs.

There's More

<u>Part 4</u>: *Sentence Puzzles* ✚✚✚ Compose sentences with different kinds of verbs. Limit your sentences to 12 words or less–keep it simple! **Also, please remember what an "o.p." is:** It's the *object of the preposition*, the noun or pronoun at the end of a prep. phrase.

7. Use a single-word verb and a prepositional phrase that includes two personal pronoun o.p.'s. If you don't remember what a personal pronoun is, flip back to p. 25 to refresh your memory!

_____

_____

8. Use a verb phrase and a prepositional phrase with a demonstrative pronoun as the o.p. If you don't remember what a demonstrative pronoun is, flip back to p. 31 to refresh your memory!

_____

_____

9. Begin with a prepositional phrase that has an indefinite pronoun for its o.p., then use a single-word verb. If you don't remember what an indefinite pronoun is, flip back to p. 30 to refresh your memory!

_____

_____

10. Use a verb phrase and a prepositional phrase that includes a reflexive pronoun for its o.p. If you don't remember what a reflexive pronoun is, flip back to p. 31 to refresh your memory!

_____

_____

11. Use a single-word verb and a verb in the infinitive form. If you don't remember what an infinitive is, flip back to p. 44 to refresh your memory!

_____

_____

12. Begin this sentence with a prepositional phrase that has two personal pronoun o.p.'s, and then use a verb phrase. If you don't remember what a personal pronoun is, flip back to p. 25 to refresh your memory!

_____

_____

PREPS for You!
(you're welcome)
about
above
across
after
against
along
around
at
before
behind
below
beneath
beside
between
beyond
by
down
during
for
from
in
in front of
inside
instead of
into
near
next to
of
off
on
out
over
through
to
toward
under
until
up
with
without

"Polluted" Verb Phrases

A. In many verb phrases, there is a word hidden among the helping and main verbs that is not actually part of the verb. When this occurs, you might say that the verb phrase is "polluted."

Example 1: Mark <u>may not meet</u> us at the movie tonight.
(Do you see the non-verb hiding inside the verb phrase?)

B. In "pure" verb phrases, each word is a helping verb or a form of some verb.

a "pure" verb phrase
Example 2: In the attic six boxes <u>will be stacked</u> near the chimney.

C. When identifying verbs in sentences, never include "polluting" words. For instance, in Example 1 above, the verb is "may meet." The word *not* is a polluting word and is not really part of the verb.

D. Here's a list of common polluting words, a.k.a. non-verbs which are often found between helping and main verbs. (When identifying verbs, <u>never</u> include these in your verb phrases!):

not never still	already almost also	words ending in **"-ly"** (usually) ex: quietly, slowly, etc.
Note: These words are adverbs. We'll discuss adverbs later.		

E. Each word in a verb phrase <u>must</u> itself be a verb, so when identifying verbs, don't include other parts of speech in the verb phrases you find.

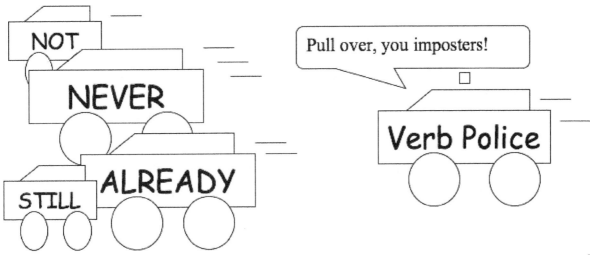

F. Look closely at the following sentence:

Bill <u>would sometimes give</u> me a bite of his candy bar.

G. Above, look at the underlined words. Only *would* and *give* are actually verbs. You can tell because *would* is on our helping verb list, and *give* is obviously a verb because it's something you can do, plus it can be changed into different forms, like a past-tense form (gave) and an "–ing" form (giving). It also has an infinitive form, "to give."

ALERT!   ALERT!   ALERT!   ALERT!

Here is some RIIYWDN *(Really Important Information You Will Definitely Need)*:

> If you are wondering if a word is a verb or even a helping verb, a good and easy test is to see if it has the kinds of different forms that verbs have.
>
> For instance, all verbs have an "–ing" form: *running, thinking, tasting*, etc. They all have past tense forms, too: *cooked, built, swung, ate, danced, lived*, etc.
>
> Even helping verbs have various forms: *can/could, will/would, may/might/must, should/shall*, etc. (Ok, fine, so *shall* isn't used much anymore, but you get the point, right?)
>
> **WATCH OUT:** The word *during* is <u>not</u> a verb. *During* is a **preposition** and is an exception.

> **Words included in a verb phrase must have the properties of a verb, i.e., various forms, especially "–ing" and past tense forms. If a word doesn't have any other verb-like forms, never include it when marking a sentence's verb.**

H. In the sentence at the top of this page, *sometimes* is not a verb. You can tell because there is no such word as "sometimes-ing," and neither is there a past tense version of *sometimes*. Therefore, *sometimes* cannot be part of the verb phrase. (*Sometimes* is an adverb.)

I. The verb in the sentence at the top of this page is "would give" with *would* functioning as a helping verb and *give* functioning as the main verb. *Sometimes* is a "polluting" word.

Mike <u>will slide</u> over next to Robin.

J. In the sentence above, both of the underlined words are forms of verbs; *will* is in our "Helping Verbs" box, plus it has another form (*would*), and *slide* also has other forms as verbs do (*sliding*, *slid*, *slides*).

K. The verb, then, is "will slide," with *will* functioning as a helping verb and *slide* functioning as the main verb.

L. Here are some more examples:

    1. Waiters must always treat their customers with the utmost courtesy.

        the verb = "must treat"

        (*Always* is not a verb, so it's not included in the verb. *Always* does not have various forms like verbs do, such as an "–ing" form or a past tense form.)

        helping verb: *must*   (It has the properties of a verb because it has various forms.)

        main verb: *treat*   (It has the properties of a verb because it has various forms.)

    2. On the crowded commuter train my father would never talk to anyone.

        the verb = "would talk"

        (*Never* is not a verb, so it's not included in the verb. It does not have various forms like verbs do, such as an "–ing" form or a past tense form.)

        helping verb: *would*   (It has the properties of a verb because it has various forms.)

        main verb: *talk*   (It has the properties of a verb because it has various forms.)

    3. The rain should still be falling after our nap.

        the verb = "should be falling"

        (*Still* is not a verb, so it's not included in the verb. It does not have various forms like verbs do, such as an "–ing" form or a past tense form.)

        helping verbs: *should*, *be*   (Both of these words have various forms; they have the properties of verbs.)

        main verb: *falling*   (It has the properties of a verb because it has various forms.)

Exercise 10

Part 1: In the blank after each sentence, write out the verb. If you find a verb phrase, don't include non-verbs when you write out the verb!

1. I may not be going to college soon. _____

2. In front of the house a tall tree created a huge patch of shade. _____

3. The boy between Jenna and me might be sleeping. _____

4. The bus did arrive at the bus stop. _____

5. Mr. Riches is still teaching at Wonderwood Middle School. _____

Part 2: Surround prepositional phrases with parentheses. A verb can never be inside a prepositional phrase, so be careful. (The blank line after each sentence is for Part 3 of this exercise.)

6. Behind Asad and her I could see three more people. _____

7. My mom went for a jog along the river walk. _____

8. I would never tell my parents a lie. _____

9. Next to my neighbor's house three purple flowers bloomed

yesterday. _____

Part 3: Go back to sentences 6, 7, 8, & 9 above and, in the blank after each sentence, write out the verb. If you find a verb phrase, don't include non-verbs in it!

There's More ➡

<u>Part 4</u>: Compose your own sentences with different kinds of verbs. Limit your sentences to 12 words or less–keep it simple!

Helping Verbs				
would could should will can	may might must	*are *am *be *been *is *was *were	*have *had *has	*do *does *did
*Multi-purpose word. Can be a helping verb, a main verb in a verb phrase, and/or even a verb all by itself.				

10. Use a single-word verb.

_____

11. Use a verb phrase that's **not** "polluted" with a non-verb.

_____

_____

12. Use a verb phrase that **is** "polluted" by a non-verb (see p. 55 for common polluting words).

_____

_____

 **Extra Practice for Evaluation 6**

<u>Part 1</u>: Surround prepositional phrases with parentheses AND underline verbs. Watch out for verb phrases and polluting words, and remember that verbs can never be inside prepositional phrases.

1. Under the bridge I am feeding the lonely ducks.

2. The recycling bin in the garage has already been emptied by Emmet.

3. During math class I dropped my pencil on the floor.

4. On the deck in my backyard two frogs were croaking in the night.

5. My sister might never be a professional surfing champion.

<u>Part 2</u>: *Sentence Puzzles* ✣➍✣ Compose your own sentences with different kinds of verbs. Limit your sentences to 12 words or less–keep it simple!

6. Begin with a prepositional phrase, then use a single-word verb. Don't forget what we talked about with intro prepositional phrases and commas!

_____

_____

7. Use a "polluted" verb phrase and three prepositional phrases.

_____

_____

8. Use a verb phrase, and include a prepositional phrase that has two objects **where both objects are personal pronouns.**

_____

_____

9. Use one introductory prepositional phrase (don't forget what we talked about with intro prep. phrases and commas!), **and** use a verb phrase.

_____

_____

 Evaluation 6: Finding Verbs + Single-Word Verbs vs. Verb Phrases – Are you ready?

BTW: There will be both Personal Pronoun & Helping Verb Refresher Boxes on the test.

Study of Action & Linking Verbs

We've already mentioned how action verbs are different from linking verbs. Now here's a recap:

A. Action Verbs

Sometimes the verb tells what the subject of a sentence does, did, or will be doing. This is when the verb is showing <u>action</u>. Verbs showing action are called Action Verbs.

Joe and Jake were playing checkers in the tent. (The subjects, Joe and Jake, were doing something—they <u>were playing</u> checkers, so "were playing" is the verb.)

B. Linking Verbs

Other times, a subject of a sentence isn't really doing anything; instead, it is just being something. In this case, the verb is called a Linking Verb because the verb <u>links</u> the subject to something the subject is being.

The waves near the reef were incredible. (*Waves* is the subject and *incredible* is what the subject was being—these words are linked by the verb *were*, a linking verb.)

The coach has been unhappy with the team's performance. (*Coach* is the subject and *unhappy* is what the subject was being—these words are linked by this sentence's verb, "has been," a linking verb.)

C. As stated earlier, one of the most important things a writer can learn regarding grammar is understanding the difference between action verbs and linking verbs because…

1. Some of the key grammar concepts yet to be learned will be much easier to apply if you can tell the difference between action and linking verbs.

2. This knowledge is also super valuable because **action verbs make for better writing, so if you can find linking verbs in your own writing, you can get rid of them and take the quality of your writing to the next level!**

How to Tell the Difference Between Linking & Action Verbs

A. Once you find a sentence's verb, there are four strategies you can use to tell if the verb is action or linking. Here are the first two strategies:

Strategy 1 **Use your common sense:** Is something happening in the sentence? Is the verb you've found something you could *do*? Is the verb you've found an "action-ee" kind of word? Remember, action verbs involve mental, emotional, and physical actions.

If the answer to any of the above questions is "yes," then you probably have an action verb. If not, the verb is most likely linking. By the way, most verbs are action verbs!

☼ *ALWAYS* apply your **common sense** *first*!

(Your common sense is a terrible thing to waste, my friend.)

Strategy 2 **Know the "classic" linking verbs** (verbs that are always linking). If the verb (or main verb of a verb phrase) is one of the "classics," then you obviously have a linking verb.

The "classic" linking verbs are:

    a. Any form of the verb "to be": *am, are, is, was, were, be, been, being*

    b. Any form of the verb "to seem": *seem, seems, seemed*

    c. Any form of the verb "to become": *become, becomes, became, becoming*

NOTE: When applying this strategy to verb phrases, look at the <u>main</u> verb—the *last* word in the verb phrase.

Helping verbs are not classified as action or linking!

Quick Practice: Mark the verbs in sentences 1-8 below like this:

Mark action verbs with a box: **At home I** ⎡colored⎤ **on the wall.**

Mark linking verbs with an "L" shape: **The boys** ⎣have been⎦ **there.**

If you find a verb phrase, be careful–do not include non-verbs in it!

Example: **After an hour the alarm ⎡was s̶t̶i̶l̶l̶ ringing.⎤**

1. The team on the bus is leaving for a tournament in California.

2. The puzzles in that book seem easy to me.

3. On Tuesday you should try the spaghetti for lunch.

4. The horse leaped over the fence near the grandstand.

5. The weather may not become nicer over the weekend.

6. The apple pie was on the kitchen counter this morning.

7. I have been to Spain to see a bullfight.

8. In the wind the trees were bending wildly.

A closer look:

    A. How many sentences above have "classic" linking verbs? _____

    B. How many sentences above have verb phrases? _____

    C. Which sentence above has a "polluting" word in it? _____

Some more strategies—ones you may need if you get into a pinch!

Strategy 3   **Replace the verb**: Replace the verb or verb phrase with a "classic" linking verb. This is a very good and popular strategy.

Examples:

This soup tastes delicious.

Replace the verb *tastes* with a form of a classic linking verb such as "to be," like *is/was*, *are/were*—whichever form of the verb best fits, such as

is
This soup ~~tastes~~ delicious.

If the meaning of the sentence <u>does not change</u>, as in the sentence above, then the original verb (*tastes*) is a linking verb.

Here's another example:

seemed
The children ~~were having~~ a great time at the party.

In this example, the meaning of the sentence <u>changes</u> when we replace the original verb, "were having," with the classic linking verb *seemed*, so "were having" is an action verb.

Strategy 4   **Sentence structure:** You can also look at the structure of the sentence. Draw a vertical line right after the verb and look at the words to the right of your line.

In linking verb sentences, after the verb you will often find a word that describes the subject of the sentence. *In action verb sentences there will not be anything after the verb that describes the subject.*

Examples:

In the afternoon the weather was becoming │ really nasty.

After the verb "was becoming," you can see that the word *nasty* describes the subject, weather. Therefore, "was becoming" is a linking verb.

Johnny ran │ three miles on the track yesterday.

After the verb *ran* there is no word that describes the subject, Johnny. Therefore, *ran* is an action verb.

Quick Practice: Mark the verbs in sentences 1-10 below like this:

Mark action verbs with a box: **Charlotte** $\boxed{\text{did score}}$ **the first point.**

Mark linking verbs with an "L" shape: **The weather** ⌐**is very breezy at the beach.**

☆ If you find a verb phrase, be careful to "x" out any non verbs you may see.

Example: **Everyone in the hallways** $\boxed{\text{is no̶i̶s̶i̶l̶y slamming}}$ **locker doors.**

1. I will probably buy three pieces of pizza at lunch.

2. She may come to your house after school next week.

3. Our new puppy snuggled between me and my dad on the couch.

4. He seemed very tall for a sixth grader.

5. In front of my house my sister parked the car.

6. Most of the guests should be on time for the ceremony tonight.

7. The celebrity chef expertly spread the icing on the vanilla cake.

8. During the speech many audience members appeared sleepy.

9. He paused for a moment at the stop sign.

10. I am not happy about this grade!

Tricky Verbs

A. Two more things worth noting here concerning action and linking verbs:

B. The verb *have* (and all of its forms) looks like a linking verb, and so, without thinking, many students mislabel it because, as main verbs or single-word verbs, all forms of the verb *have* are ACTION verbs!

> **He has a huge headache.** (*Has* is the verb, and it's an ACTION verb.)

> **We will be having turkey for dinner tonight.** ("Will be having" is the verb, and since the main verb is a form of the verb *have*, "will be having" is an ACTION verb.)

By the way, applying strategies 3 & 4 (p. 64) confirms the fact that the verbs above are action verbs.

C. The "sense" words—*look*, *feel*, *sound*, *taste*, and *smell*—can be linking or action verbs depending on how they are used. Of course, they look like sure action verbs, but many times they are not action verbs, so they are also often mislabeled.

> **The chef tasted the soup.** (*Tasted* is an <u>action</u> verb here because the subject, chef, is actually doing something.)

> **The soup tasted delicious.** (In this sentence, *tasted* is a <u>linking</u> verb because the subject, soup, isn't doing anything—it's just being delicious.)

☆ Don't jump to conclusions about action/linking based on what a verb looks like!

D. Below, check the box next to the sentence where *looks* is an Action Verb:

> [ ] **That dress looks really fancy.**

> [ ] **My mom always looks through the sale rack first.**

(Did you check the right box?)

This is a VERY IMPORTANT page—you should bookmark it and be sure to review it before the next evaluation!

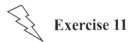

Exercise 11

<u>Part 1</u>: Surround prepositional phrases with parentheses. Verbs can never be inside prepositional phrases, so be careful.

1. I did receive several awards at my graduation.

2. Until noon all of the burgers will be served by the Girl Scouts.

3. Against all odds my team won the championship of our league.

4. On the sidelines the coach looked terribly nervous.

5. At the game you might feel chilly without a coat or a hat.

6. After college Zayd would soon become a great scientist.

7. Jill can take a seat by them along the aisle.

8. Over the break I will have my twelfth birthday party at the beach.

9. To Melinda and me the test seemed really tough.

10. That goat may not eat the food from your hand.

<u>Part 2</u>: Go back to sentences 1-10 above and mark action verbs with a box and linking verbs with an "L" shape. **Reminder:** If you find a verb phrase, be careful—do not include non-verbs in it!

Humor Break!

The teacher asked the little girl if she would be going to the dance. "No, I ain't going" was the reply.

The teacher corrected the child: "You must not say, 'I ain't going.' You must say, 'I am not going.'" She continued in order to press the point: "I am not going. He is not going. We are not going. You are not going. They are not going. Now, dear, can you say all that?"

The little girl nodded and smiled brightly. "Sure!" she replied. "There ain't nobody going!"

Extra Practice for Evaluation 7

<u>Part 1</u>: Surround prepositional phrases with parentheses in sentences 1-5. Verbs can never be inside prepositional phrases, so be careful.

1. The snake slid through the grass near the porch.

2. Everyone on my bus laughed loudly at my hilarious joke.

3. The pencils under the desk were spilled by Melissa.

4. Your sandwich from the deli is next to that soda can.

5. The weeds along the fence have grown to my knees.

<u>Part 2</u>: In the sentences above as well as the sentences below, mark action verbs with a box; mark linking verbs with an "L" shape. **Reminder:** If you find a polluted verb phrase, "X" out the non-verbs!

6. In front of the room Carlotta did find three large tables.

7. I had never run a race against you.

8. The napkins do not have pretty flower designs on them.

9. Ten jellybeans might be rolling around under the table.

10. During the movie children had quietly sipped their sodas.

11. To Kenyon and me everyone at the school seemed very polite.

12. Must you bother us during this TV show?

13. This award can be presented to Julia and him on Sunday.

Helping Verbs
would
could
should
will
can
may
might
must
*are
*am
*be
*been
*is
*was
*were
*have
*had
*has
*do
*does
*did
*Multi-purpose word. Can also be a main verb in a verb phrase and/or even a verb all by itself.

Part 3: *Sentence Puzzles* ✚✚✚ Compose your own sentences with different kinds of verbs. Limit your sentences to 12 words or less–keep it simple!

14. Use a verb phrase that is a linking verb.

_____

_____

15. Use a single-word verb that is an action verb, and include a prepositional phrase that has two personal pronoun o.p.'s.

_____

_____

16. Use a single-word verb that is a linking verb.

_____

_____

17. Use a verb phrase that is an action verb.

_____

_____

Part 4: List the four strategies you can use to determine if a verb is action or linking.

18. _____

19. _____

20. _____

21. _____

➤ **Evaluation 7: Action Verb vs. Linking Verb + Single-Word Verbs vs. Verb Phrases**
– Are you ready now?

BTW: There will be both Helping Verb & Personal Pronoun Refresher Boxes on the test.

Chapter 4

Verbs & Writing

A. Now that you've had some experience with verbs in a grammatical way, it's time to use that knowledge to improve your writing!

B. Good writers are very skilled with their verbs. They know how powerful good verb usage is. So, what are the most-important things to learn about verb usage?

C. There are three main ways a person can improve his or her writing through attention to verbs:

1. **Limit the use of helping verbs.**

2. **Use action verbs rather than linking verbs** whenever possible.

3. **Use the "active voice" in your writing.** In other words, when using action verbs, make sure that the subject of the sentence is doing the action.

Rest in peace, boiling water. You will be mist!
©Richbaub's Ink Works

Limiting the Use of Helping Verbs

A. Helping verbs are often unnecessary. Consider the underlined verbs in the following sentences:

    1. **As Tom slept, the cat <u>was napping</u> on the windowsill.**

    2. **As Tom slept, the cat <u>napped</u> on the windowsill.**

Is there any difference in meaning between sentences 1 and 2?

Good writers know that using extra, unnecessary words is a no-no! Therefore, sentence 2 above is better writing than sentence 1.

B. Helping verbs are necessary sometimes. They can put verbs into just the right tense. In one of the sentences below, the helping verb *has* plays an important role.

    1. **Sheila <u>has run</u> in many marathons.**

    2. **Sheila <u>runs</u> in many marathons.**

<u>Sentence 1</u> states that Sheila has, in the past, run marathons. It also implies that she may or may not run marathons anymore. <u>Sentence 2</u> states that Sheila has run and still runs marathons.

C. The point is to recognize helping verbs in your writing and eliminate them whenever it's possible to do so.

Sir Lancelot with his lesser-known brother, Sir Render.

Exercise 12

<u>Directions</u>: Read the following passage. If you notice any unnecessary helping verbs (or other unnecessary words), cross them out. You may need to adjust the endings of verbs, too. **Different writers will make different choices, so just do your best!**

Yesterday Hugh was running in the park when he noticed something shiny that was sitting on one of the park benches along his route. He didn't think much of it, but when he had returned to his apartment, his curiosity about the object he had seen glimmering on that park bench was beginning to really bother him. He decided to go back and check it out.

As he was approaching the bench, he noticed that an old woman was now sitting on the bench near where he had seen the shiny object. He was wondering if the object had belonged to her. Suddenly, she stood up, turned, and, with a huge smile on her face, walked off. Her clothes were tattered and filthy, but a giant diamond ring was sparkling on her left hand!

©Richbaub's
Ink Works

Using Action Verbs Rather Than Linking Verbs

A. Beginning writers often overuse linking verbs like *was*, *is*, *were*, *are*, etc. Avoiding the over-use of such words should be a goal for all writers.

B. Linking verbs relate information in the least visual way. Writing comes alive when authors use words to plant images in readers' minds, and action verbs have the power to do this!

For example:

    1. Joe <u>was</u> at the bus stop for twenty minutes.

    2. Joe <u>stood</u> at the bus stop for twenty minutes.

Above, the verb *stood* relays an image to the reader. It's not an incredibly descriptive action verb, but the linking verb *was* relates nothing, and the reader is left to wonder if Joe is slouching, sitting, reading, napping, shivering, or whatever… Don't force your readers to do all of this wondering!

C. Some verbs are better than others. Even some action verbs are overused. Your challenge as a writer is to pick the verb that most-accurately describes to your reader what you see in your mind when you're composing a sentence.

For example:

    1. Jaclyn <u>took</u> a book from her locker and ran to class.

    2. Jaclyn <u>grabbed</u> a book from her locker and ran to class.

Above, both sentences have action verbs. Which sentence is better? Why?

D. In summary, limiting linking verbs and choosing interesting action verbs WILL improve your writing!

Exercise 13

Part 1: In the following sentences cross out the linking verbs and replace them with action verbs. You may need to cross out more than just the linking verb in some sentences, and in some cases you may even have to add a few words. Hint: Give the subject something to do!

1. This morning Tara was in the backyard.

2. The guests were upset at their waiter.

3. The summer sun is high in the sky at noon.

4. Under the waves near the beach were schools of silver fish.

5. During the lecture several students became very sleepy.

Part 2: In the following sentences put a box around each verb (they're all action verbs). In the spaces under each sentence, suggest **better action verbs** that could replace the original verb. **If you can also eliminate helping verbs, then do so.**

6. Behind the security guard the thief was walking toward the vault.

_____ , _____ , _____

7. Manny looked through his notebook for his missing assignment.

_____ , _____ , _____

8. On Fridays we usually have pizza for dinner.

_____ , _____ , _____

9. Will you please get that hat for me?

_____ , _____ , _____

10. In the wild, wolves will follow their prey sometimes for days.

_____ , _____ , _____

(Do you know why sentence 8 has no comma after its introductory prep. phrase, but sentence 10 does?)

Richbaub's Introduction to Middle School Grammar **Third Edition** © 2023 Richbaub's Ink Works *all rights reserved*

Using the Active Voice in Your Writing

A. When using action verbs, **make sure that the main person or thing your sentence is about (the subject) is doing the action**.

For example:

1. The <u>ball was kicked</u> through the goalposts by Junior.

The focus (subject) of sentence 1 is the ball, but the ball didn't do anything—something was done *to* it. It was Junior who actually did something. Therefore, Junior and what he did should be the subject of the sentence:

2. <u>Junior kicked</u> the ball through the goalposts.

B. Above, sentence 1 is an example of "passive voice" writing because the grammatical subject of the sentence, ball, is not doing what the verb says ("was kicked"). The person who did the kicking is buried in a later prepositional phrase.

Sentence 2 is written in the preferable "active voice." Active voice means that the sentence is organized so that the person or thing doing what the verb says is in the subject position. Passive voice writing is not incorrect, and there are certainly times when it works just fine, but active voice writing is often the better choice.

C. You may notice that when you pay attention to eliminating helping verbs, you sometimes end up changing a sentence around from passive to active voice.

Examples:

Passive Voice:

Dinner <u>was served</u> to us by a bearded man in a velvet jacket.

Active Voice:

A bearded man in a velvet jacket <u>served</u> us dinner.

D. So think "active voice" when writing. Create sentences where the subjects actually *do* something!

Exercise 14

<u>Part 1</u>: Write "A" or "P" in the blank before each sentence depending on whether the sentence is written in the active (A) or passive (P) voice.

_____ 1. The baby frog was handed to Mike by the science teacher.

_____ 2. During the thunderstorm the child cried for his mommy.

_____ 3. The surfer was easily flipped over by the massive wave.

_____ 4. Maya planted a giant sunflower outside her bedroom window.

<u>Part 2</u>: Using the given verbs and prepositional phrases, construct sentences written in the active voice. Try to limit your sentences to 12 words or less, and don't forget to try to avoid using any helping verbs.

5. chased   up the tree

_____

_____

6. hit   over the fence

_____

_____

7. protected   in the cedar chest *(this is a tough one!)*

_____

_____

8. planned   by my parents

_____

_____

Incredible Crossword Puzzle

Complete the puzzle to review some of the terms we've studied so far!

Across

2. in a verb phrase, the last word
3. a verb that's composed of more than one word
5. helps a main verb get into the right tense
12. a group of words beginning with a preposition and ending with a noun or pronoun
14. try not to use one after a single introductory prepositional phrase
15. *to* plus a verb
16. subs in for a noun sometimes

Down

1. the last word in a prepositional phrase
4. imagine pointing when trying to remember *these* (a type of pronoun!)
6. the pronouns that end with *–selves* or *–self*
7. begins a phrase that ends with an o.p.
8. this pronoun type includes words like *everyone*, *many*, *several*, and *few*
9. tells you what the subject is doing, or links subject to a word that describes what the subject is being
10. a connecting word, such as *and* or *but*
11. person, place, thing, or idea
13. these pronouns have rules—some can be used in prepositional phrases, and some cannot

Chapter 5

Subjects

In addition to topics like active/passive voice writing discussed in the previous chapter, plenty of punctuation and usage rules require an understanding of subjects, too. For instance, certain pronouns can never be used as subjects. Did you know that you can never use me as a subject?

As you become a more advanced writer, a knowledge of subjects will come into play when learning all about phrases and clauses because the major difference between a phrase and a clause is that one has a subject and a verb and one doesn't.

How about this: Do you know what a compound sentence is? You should, because there is an important punctuation situation involved with compound sentences—and knowing about subjects is a key to recognizing a compound sentence.

Study of Subjects

A. As stated earlier, a subject is the main person or thing a sentence is about. Subjects are always nouns or pronouns.

B. Most sentences have one subject, but many have two subjects, and some sentences have three or more. Examples:

> 1. The test in social studies is very difficult.
> **Subject** = *test*
>
> 2. My aunt and uncle live in New Jersey.
> **Subjects** = *aunt, uncle* (The word *and* is not part of the subject—it's one of those connecting words called conjunctions.)
>
> 3. Around the corner two thieves are robbing a bank!
> **Subject** = *thieves*
>
> 4. My ankles, feet, and toes were sore after the marathon.
> **Subjects** = *ankles, feet, toes*

Can you pick out the verbs in the sentences above? (Write each down on the given lines.)	Can you tell if each is an action or linking verb? (Circle one for each verb.)	
1. _____	AV	LV
2. _____	AV	LV
3. _____	AV	LV
4. _____	AV	LV

The Relationship Between Subjects & Verbs

A. Subjects "belong" to verbs. The subject is the person or thing that is doing or being what the verb says.

B. Do you remember how to find the verb? Make the sentence say the opposite… (See p. 52.)

C. To find a verb's subject, first locate the verb, then ask, "Who or what _____?"
(insert verb)

Examples:

    1. At the picnic on Saturday everyone $\boxed{\text{loved}}$ **the fried chicken.**

        "Who or what *loved*?" Answer = *everyone*, so *everyone* is the subject

    2. My grandmother $\boxed{\text{sat}}$ **near the window in her room.**

        "Who or what *sat*?" Answer = *grandmother*, so *grandmother* is the subject

    3. The brother and sister $\boxed{\text{had}}$ **similar smiles.**

        "Who or what *had*?" Answer = *brother*, *sister* (two subjects in this sentence)

    4. The construction workers $\boxed{\text{are}}$ **at the corner of my block.**

        "Who or what *are*?" Answer = *workers*

D. Notice that the subject in #4 above is NOT "construction workers." How come?

    Subjects are nouns and pronouns only—they do NOT include things that describe the subject… *Construction* describes the noun *workers*, so *construction* is **not** part of the subject.

E. Also, subjects are NEVER inside prepositional phrases. What's the subject in the following sentence?

At the restaurant all of the boys ordered fried chicken.

    Write your answer here: _____ (Were you correct?)

Exercise 15

Part 1: Surround prepositional phrases with parentheses.

1. Beneath a layer of snow three little eggs were found by Michael.

2. The woman near my dad and me did carry three large bundles.

3. At night she and I would never watch movies about scary things.

4. A snake might slowly slither between the rocks at my feet.

5. The sky should become dark before the rainfall.

Part 2: In the sentences above, mark action verbs with boxes and linking verbs with "L" shapes. Be careful of "polluted" verb phrases, and do you remember that verbs are never found inside prepositional phrases?

Part 3: Now circle the subjects in the sentences—but be careful because, like verbs, subjects are NEVER found inside prepositional phrases.

Part 4: Circle the subjects in the sentences below. Remember, subjects are NEVER found inside prepositional phrases.

6. On the mountain top, a coyote will often howl at the moon.

7. I am going to the beach with Anders.

8. None of the boys in the back row are very tall kids.

9. For example, the girls are standing in the front of the line.

10. Does our p.e. coach require us to run three laps on Mondays?

(Do you know why sentence 6 has a comma after an intro prep. phrase and sentence 3 does not?)

Humor Break!

"I don't need none," shouted the lady of the house even before the young man at the door had a chance to say anything.

"How do you know, lady?" he said. "I just might be selling grammar books."

Analyzing the Locations of Subjects in Sentences

A. It's important to begin to pay attention to sentence patterns!

B. For example, verbs are usually in the middle of a sentence, so when you're looking for verbs, look there.

> At the park Sheena **played** with her new puppy.

C. As far as subjects are concerned, most come <u>before</u> the verb. Understanding basic sentence patterns will save you time when analyzing the parts of a sentence.

> The **players** jogged from the gym to the field.

D. Also, subjects and prepositional phrases don't mix! Subjects are NEVER inside prepositional phrases.

> A **few** of my relatives live in Peru.

E. Therefore, before you set out to locate a sentence's subject, surround each prepositional phrase so that you know not to look there. Many times, if you mark the prepositional phrases, there aren't too many words left that could be the subject, which makes your search for the subject easier.

Some common sentence "formulas":

$$(\quad) + S + V + (\quad)$$

$$S + (\quad) + V + (\quad)$$

$$S + V + (\quad) + (\quad)$$

Can you match these formulas with the example sentences above? Try it!

 **Exercise 16**

<u>Part 1</u>: Surround prepositional phrases with parentheses.

1. Everyone in my class is doing well on the math tests.

2. For many people thunder can sound scary.

3. Selena and James would never have their homework on time.

4. Most of the questions on the test were really easy.

5. The gift from her and him must have been wrapped by their mom.

<u>Part 2</u>: In the sentences above, mark action verbs with boxes and linking verbs with "L" shapes. Be careful of "polluted" verb phrases, and do you remember that verbs are never found inside prepositional phrases?

<u>Part 3</u>: Now circle the subjects in the sentences above—but be careful because, like verbs, subjects are NEVER found inside prepositional phrases.

<u>Part 4</u>: Circle the subjects in the sentences below. Remember, subjects are NEVER found inside prepositional phrases.

6. Several of my friends may come over to my house over the holiday.

7. Sarah and I haven't met the new family across the street.

8. The gas station does glow on the deserted midnight highway.

9. Between my dad and me crept a greasy little rat.
   (What is unusual about this sentence?)

10. Do you or your brother ever read in your beds at night?

 Richbaub's Introduction to Middle School Grammar **Third Edition** © 2023 Richbaub's Ink Works *all rights reserved*

Extra Practice for Evaluation 8

Part 1: Surround prepositional phrases with parentheses, then mark action verbs with boxes and linking verbs with "L" shapes. Verbs can never be inside prepositional phrases, so be careful.

1. At nap time she sat on the bed and comforted the tiny baby.

2. For a long time the line did not move at all.

3. My aunt and uncle gave giant beach towels to my brother and me.

4. The greyhounds should be chasing the bunny around the track.

5. You or I have never had a turtle in a box for a pet.

6. The sound seemed to fade in the distance.

Part 2: In sentences 1-6, circle the subjects. Remember—subjects are never found inside prepositional phrases.

Part 3: *Sentence Puzzles* ✲╫✲ Write sentences as directed. Limit your sentences to 15 words or less–keep it simple!

7. Begin with a prepositional phrase, and use a verb phrase that is a linking verb.

_____

_____

8. Use a single-word verb that is a linking verb and two prepositional phrases.

_____

9. Use a "polluted" verb phrase that is an action verb, and include three prepositional phrases. (See common polluting words on p. 85.)

_____

Helping Verbs
would
could
should
will
can
may
might
must
*are
*am
*be
*been
*is
*was
*were
*have
*had
*has
*do
*does
*did
*Multi-purpose word. Can also be a main verb in a verb phrase and/or even a verb all by itself.

 Evaluation 8: Subjects + Action Verbs vs. Linking Verbs – Are you ready now?

BTW: There will be both Classic Linking Verbs & Helping Verb Refresher Boxes on the test.

Personal Pronouns & Subjects

A. As you know, a subject is either a noun or a pronoun. But what you might not know is that there are rules for using certain pronouns as subjects.

B. Do you remember when we discussed Personal Pronouns and prepositional phrases? Well, it's those Personal Pronouns again. Some can <u>never</u> be used as subjects.

C. Once more, here are the Personal Pronouns:

Objective Case Personal Pronouns	Nominative Case Personal Pronouns
me	I
you	you
her	she
it	it
him	he
us	we
them	they
whom	who

As you can see, *you* and *it* are both objective <u>and</u> nominative case personal pronouns. They are "all-purpose" personal pronouns.

Do the phrases
Mr. Tummes
and
TIE EYE UO
ring a bell?

D. What's most important here is that when using Personal Pronouns as subjects, you MUST choose a word from the <u>Nominative</u> Case Personal Pronouns list.

E. This is different from prepositional phrases—in prepositional phrases you must use only <u>Objective</u> Case Personal Pronouns.

F. Again, for <u>subjects</u>, when using Personal Pronouns, you may **only** use <u>Nominative</u> Case Personal Pronouns.

Exercise 17

In this exercise you will use personal pronouns:

Objective Case Personal Pronouns	Nominative Case Personal Pronouns
me	I
you	you
her	she
it	it
him	he
us	we
them	they
whom	who

As you can see, *you* and *it* are both objective <u>and</u> nominative case personal pronouns. They are "all-purpose" personal pronouns that can be used anywhere.

Part 1: *Sentence Puzzles* ✚✚✚ Write sentences as directed.

Write two sentences that each have a personal pronoun for a subject and a prepositional phrase with a <u>personal pronoun o.p.</u> (object of the preposition). Limit your sentences to 12 words or less–keep it simple!

1. _____

_____

2. **(Use a verb phrase in this sentence.)** _____

_____

Write two sentences that each have two subjects where BOTH are personal pronouns. Limit your sentences to 12 words or less.

Common Polluting Words
not
never
still
already
almost
also
-ly words

3. _____

_____

4. **(Use a polluted verb phrase in this sentence.)** _____

_____

Part 2: In the following sentences, fill each blank line with a personal pronoun. Don't use *you* or *it*—that would be too easy!

5. _____ and my dad enjoy fishing on Saturday mornings.

6. After school _____ and _____ are going shopping at the mall.

7. _____ and _____ were excited about making the baseball team.

8. At the beach Joe and _____ were playing in a volleyball tournament.

<u>Part 3</u>: In sentences below, fix any personal pronouns used incorrectly.

9. Toward the end of the day Ted and him headed for the swimming pool.

10. The spider landed in front of she and Amina.

11. Neither of the boys will have cake with Remy and I.

12. By who will you sit during the play this afternoon?

Multiple Subjects, Multiple Verbs, & Compound Sentences

A. The following sentences both have two subjects and two verbs, but they are very different kinds of sentences.

    a. Constance and her sister stopped at a restaurant and ate dinner.

    b. David needed some bread, but the grocery store had already closed.

B. The main difference between the two sentences above is that sentence "a" cannot easily be split into two sentences. Sentence "b," on the other hand, actually contains two <u>independent clauses</u>.

C. An independent clause is a group of words that includes a subject and a verb that can stand on its own as a complete sentence. It would be very easy to break sentence "b" into two separate, complete sentences. Do you see the two independent clauses in sentence "b"? (David needed some bread/the grocery store had already closed)

D. Sentence "b" is called a <u>compound sentence</u> because inside of it there are the makings of two separate and complete sentences; two independent clauses have simply been joined together into a single sentence.

E. Which of the following sentences are **compound sentences**?

    1. The snake hissed and slithered around my math workbook.

    2. My jeans got dirty, so I put them in the laundry.

    3. Meredith has excellent grades, and she is a fabulous soccer player.

    4. In front of my house a truck lost control and skidded into a ditch.

Pi Thon

Punctuating Compound Sentences

A. It's important to be able to recognize compound sentences because there's a punctuation rule for them:

> **When you join two separate sentences (independent clauses) together to form a compound sentence, you must use either a <u>comma and a conjunction</u> OR a <u>semi-colon</u> (;) to make the connection.**

B. Most often, a compound sentence is formed with a comma and one of the following conjunctions:

for
and
nor
but
or
yet
so

> Do you know why many refer to these conjunctions as the FANBOYS??

> The word *for* is a conjunction when it's being used to connect sentences. When it begins a prepositional phrase, it's a preposition.

C. These connecting words are called *coordinating conjunctions* and are often referred to by the acronym "fanboys."

D. Once again, join two independent clauses with <u>a comma and a conjunction</u> OR a <u>semi-colon</u>:

> **FYI**
>
> Independent clauses joined without punctuation are called **"run-on"** sentences.
> A **"comma splice"** error is where independent clauses are joined with *only* a comma.

   a. My soup was too hot**, so** I put an ice cube in it.

   b. Basketball is a fun sport**, but** it is very tiring.

   c. My sister ordered a sandwich**, and** my dad ordered a salad.

   d. Our neighbors traveled to Disney World**;** my family stayed home.

E. When a sentence has more than one subject and/or more than one verb but does not contain two independent clauses, do NOT use a comma and a conjunction or a semi-colon:

   1. The skydiver jumped out of the plane and tumbled toward the earth.

   2. The lizards and snakes at the zoo frightened my mom.

   3. Thomas and his dog jumped out of the car and headed for the beach.

Exercise 18

Part 1: Write two compound sentences. Limit each sentence to 15 words or less, and be sure to use the correct punctuation.

1. _____

_____

2. **(Use a verb phrase in this sentence.)** _____

_____

Part 2: Insert commas or semi-colons <u>where needed</u>. Some sentences will not need any punctuation added. On the line after each sentence, explain why you added (for example "it is compound," "I see two independent clauses," etc.) or did not add punctuation ("there's only one sentence," etc.).

3. Before the game I stretched my legs and warmed up my arm.

_____

4. Tina's uncle bought two Super Bowl tickets and gave them to Tina and me.

_____

5. The bear cubs looked lost hopefully their mother will find them soon.

_____

6. We needed a time out for our defense looked confused.

_____

7. In the cabinet next to the refrigerator I may find some cereal and pour myself a bowl.

_____

8. He and I will be on the same flight so we will arrive in Orlando together.

_____

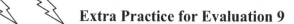

Part 1: Surround prepositional phrases with parentheses, mark action verbs with boxes and linking verbs with "L" shapes, AND circle subjects.

1. For summer vacation you should always go to the beach.

2. My dad and I played soccer against the neighborhood kids.

3. Some of my teammates were wearing long blue socks.

4. I travelled down the road, and I saw three turtles in a pond.

5. Those burgers on the grill smell delicious.

6. The problems on page six seem too difficult for me and Mike.

Part 2: Fix personal pronouns used incorrectly.

7. The alligator slowly crawled toward my mom and I.

8. The Walkers and us arrived before Lisa and him.

9. From California we drove north for a scenic journey with she and my uncle.

Part 3: Insert commas or semi-colons if needed.

10. Around eight o'clock we went to the porch and my mom made us a cup of hot chocolate.

11. Sally and Terence joined the team and quickly became our best players.

12. For lunch we had grilled cheese sandwiches we didn't have time for dessert.

Part 4: *Sentence Puzzles* ✚✚✚   Write sentences as directed, and, please, keep it simple!

13. Write a compound sentence that includes three prepositional phrases (not necessarily in a row!) and two different verb phrases.

_____

_____

14. Write a sentence that includes one verb and two subjects where BOTH subjects are personal pronouns.

_____

_____

15. Write a sentence that includes two verbs and a prepositional phrase with two personal pronoun o.p.'s.

_____

_____

   Evaluation 9: Finding Subjects and Using Personal Pronouns as Subjects + Punctuating Compound Sentences – Are you ready now?

BTW: There will be a Personal Pronoun Refresher Box on the test.

Chapter 6

Punctuating Dialogue

*Have you read any books lately? Well, if you have, and I assume that you have, then you know that dialogue is
ALL OVER THE PLACE!*

*The funny (scary?) thing is, however, that even though you constantly see dialogue in the books you read, many
students STILL don't realize that two people can NEVER speak in the same paragraph, that there is ALWAYS
punctuation at the end of a quotation, or that words like said are NEVER capitalized.*

Seriously, you need to pay attention to the info in this chapter!

Introduction to Punctuating Dialogue

A. "Dialogue" means that two or more people are speaking to each other. Writers often
record what other people say, so it's important to know how to correctly punctuate dialogue in
your writing.

B. Even when you're recording what just one person said or is saying, you need to
punctuate it in a certain way.

C. Quotation marks are only part of the punctuation you will need when quoting someone.
You also need commas and end marks, such as periods, in just the right places. Paying attention
to upper and lower-case letters is also important.

JUST the RIGHT PLACE!!

Tired of being in
all the wrong places,
some brave punctuation
marks decide to make
a change.

Let's go!

©Richbaub's
Ink Works

Richbaub's Introduction to Middle School Grammar **Third Edition**

Quotation Marks in Dialogue

A. Quotation marks (" ") are used at the beginning and end of a quotation. They surround what someone says.

Examples:

1. "Fish swim," said Joe.

2. Joe said, "I like white bread. I also like flour tortillas."

B. Notice that quotation marks do not go around each sentence someone says. They start when someone begins to speak, and they're not used again until he or she is finished speaking.

C. Sometimes single quotation marks are used. Single quotation marks, however, are <u>only</u> used with a quotation inside of another quotation.

Example:

Will said, "I love it when the baby says, 'Goo goo.' It really makes me laugh!"

D. **Quick Practice** – Add quotation marks to the following dialogue:

Mom said , Will you be home early tonight ?

Dad said , I don't think so . I've got to finish a project .

I said , You work too much , Dad . We miss you !

But this morning you said , I'll take you guys to a movie tonight , said my brother .

Dad said , I'm sorry . I'll make it up to you this weekend .

Commas, Periods, & Other End Marks in Dialogue

A. Look at the end marks (periods, exclamation points, and question marks) and commas in the following exchange between Robert and Teresa:

"You told me I could buy this candy bar for one dollar," said Robert.

Teresa replied, "That's not what I said. I said it costs two dollars!"

"Really?" said Robert.

"Yes, really!" said Teresa.

B. At the end of every quotation there is some sort of punctuation, and this punctuation is always placed **inside** the quotation marks, whether it's a comma, period, exclamation point, or question mark.

C. In the second line of dialogue above, there is a comma before the quotation because it's introduced by "Teresa replied." Always use a comma when introducing a quotation with something like "Bob said" or "Joe asked," etc.

D. **Quick Practice** – Add commas and end marks to the following dialogue:

Max said " Do you like peanut butter "

" No, I do not like peanut butter " answered Ann

" Then I guess we can't be friends " said Max

Surprised, Ann said " Wow. You must really love peanut

butter "

Capital & Lowercase Letters in Dialogue

A. When beginning a quotation, always capitalize the first letter of the first word of the quotation—even if the quotation begins in the middle of a sentence.

Examples:

"**F**ish swim," said Joe.

Joe said, "**F**ish swim."

B. Words like *said, asked, exclaimed, stated,* etc. are **never** capitalized in dialogue—even when they come after an exclamation point or question mark.

Examples:

"We rock!" **e**xclaimed Joe.

"Do bugs sleep?" **a**sked Alex.

"Rain is coming," **s**aid the weatherman.

C. **Quick practice** – Fill in the missing letters. Pay attention to whether they should be capitalized or not.

Joe __aid, "__hy don't you come over to my house today?"

"__o, I can't," __aid Kent.

"__hy not?" __aid Joe.

Kent replied, "__ecause my mom said I have to do homework!"

Interrupted Quotations

A. Sometimes authors don't begin or end a quotation by identifying the speaker. Sometimes authors make a break in the middle of a quotation to let the reader know who's speaking. Compare the following:

1. Joe said, "Pie is good, but cake is totally awesome!"

2. "Lemons are yellow. Bananas are yellow, too," said Joe.

3. "Pie is good," said Joe, "but cake is totally awesome!"

4. "Lemons are yellow," said Joe. "Bananas are yellow, too."

Above, lines 3 and 4 feature **interrupted quotations** because "said Joe" comes right in the middle of Joe speaking—not before or after he speaks as in examples 1 and 2.

B. With interrupted quotations the punctuation and capitalization are a little bit tricky. For instance, examples 3 and 4 above look very similar, but after "said Joe" the punctuation and capital letter usage is different. Here are the examples again:

3. "Pie is good," said Joe, "but cake is totally awesome."

4. "Lemons are yellow," said Joe. "Bananas are yellow, too."
⇧ ⇧

Why is the punctuation and capital letter usage different where the arrows point?

C. In example 3, "said Joe" is completely interrupting a sentence—and so when you pick the sentence back up after "said Joe" with the word *but*, you go with a comma and a lower-case letter.

D. In example 4, "said Joe" is actually between two separate sentences. In this case, you put a period after "said Joe" to conclude the first sentence. After "said Joe" a new sentence begins with the word *bananas*, so you go with a capital letter as Joe continues to speak.

E. **Quick Practice** - Fill in the missing letters (L) and punctuation (P). Pay attention to whether letters should be capitalized or not.

"__et's meet after school__" __aid Tim__ "__o we can work on the project."
  L   P   L   P   L

"I can't__" __aid Tonya __ "__y mom can't drive me then."
        P   L   P   L

Tim __aid__ "__y mom can pick you up."
    L   P   L

"__reat__" __aid Tonya __ "__re you sure that's ok?"
 L   P   L   P   L

"No problem!" __aid Tim.
              L

Gift Rap

Multiple Speakers & Paragraph Breaks

A. When you record a conversation, change to a new paragraph when you switch to a different character:

> "Let's go to the beach today," said Marcus. "It's too hot to play in the neighborhood."
>
> "Great idea, Marcus," said Louis. "We should call David. He's a great surfer, and I'm sure he would love to come with us." Louis grabbed his phone and began entering David's number.
>
> "Wait!" said Marcus. "I just remembered that David is away on vacation. Let's call Tracey and Meredith instead." Marcus paused. Louis had a funny look on his face, almost like he was suddenly scared of something.
>
> After gulping, Louis finally began to speak. "Tracey and Meredith? Aren't those the girls who just moved here from Hawaii? You know," Louis continued, "they might be better surfers than we are!"
>
> With a sly smile Marcus said, "Scared of a little competition, Lou?"

B. Notice that paragraphs of dialogue can contain a combination of quotation and narration (the narrator speaking). Every line of quoted dialogue doesn't necessarily get its own paragraph; you only must move to a new paragraph when a different character is quoted. No single paragraph should include quotations from two different characters!

C. The forced paragraph breaks come in handy, too, because with long conversations authors can drop the "he saids" and "she saids" since the paragraph breaks signal that the speaker has changed.

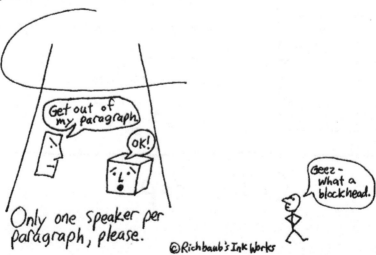

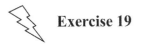 **Exercise 19**

<u>Directions</u>: The following chart contains quotations from a dialogue involving Kevin, James, and their mom.

On the following page, re-write everything in paragraph form using the rules we've discussed about punctuating dialogue.

Not only will you add punctuation and paragraph breaks, but you will also add "Kevin said" and "said James," etc. each time someone speaks. Where you put "James said" and "said Kevin" can vary, so mix it up a little!

Begin the dialogue with Kevin, and then alternate between the speakers in a way that makes the most sense.

What Kevin said	What James said	What Mom said
Mom says we have to clean up our room before we can go to the game tonight.	It's mostly your mess.	Boys? Jamie just called, and she'll be here to pick you up for the game in five minutes. How does your room look?
That's not true. You haven't made your bed for two weeks!	At least I put my clothes away. You, on the other hand, just leave your old clothes wherever you happen to be standing when you undress. You're a total slob, dude!	
Are you blind? Your homework desk is covered with Doritos crumbs!		
	Oh no!	
Crud!		

Write the dialogue out on the next page. ⎯⎯⎯⎯⎯⎯⟶

Re-write the dialogue here (begin with Kevin):

_____

_____

_____

_____

_____

_____

_____

_____

_____

_____

_____

_____

_____

Extra Practice for Evaluation 10

Directions: Read through the following dialogue and put a ✓ next to the lines that have NO errors. For lines with errors, leave the line blank, but do correct the mistake(s) in the line.

1. _____   One summer day a trout approached a young boy sitting

2. _____   on a dock. "Hey, little boy," said the trout, "The bait you're

3. _____   using is quite delicious, but my friends and family are having a

4. _____   hard time avoiding your sharp hook."

5. _____   Startled for a moment, the boy slowly replied "Really?

6. _____   Then how come I haven't caught any of you?"

7. _____   "We are much more clever than you think, little boy" said

8. _____   the trout, "Your hook does from time to time injure us, though.

9. _____   "My little son Jimmy was pricked just a moment ago as he

10. _____   nibbled on your bait."

11. _____   "I knew I'd felt a bite!" Said the little boy.

12. _____   "Indeed. Which brings me to the purpose of this little

13. _____   visit", said the trout.

14. _____   The little boy frowned and said, "Yes, why exactly are

15. _____   you talking to me anyway?" The trout became a bit frightened

16. _____   by the little boy's stern face and glanced away toward the

17. _____   surface of the lake where his family and friends were looking up

18. _____   at him. He regained his courage.

19. _____   "It's just that, well, we're still hungry, and your hook is

20. _____   now empty," said the trout. "could you please put some more

21. _____   bait on for us? We would much appreciate it"!

 Evaluation 10: Punctuating Dialogue – Are you ready?

Chapter 7

Adjectives

Understanding adjectives goes WAY beyond knowing about the words that describe nouns and pronouns!

First of all, there's a certain type of adjective which you've probably never heard of: the predicate adjective. You'll be learning about predicate adjectives and their close cousins, predicate nominatives. Understanding these descriptive words will add to your knowledge about when to use me *vs. when to use* I *(and all of the other personal pronouns).*

Secondly, as you become a more advanced writer, you will discover groups of words—phrases and clauses—that also function as adjectives. Knowing about adjective phrases and clauses will add a whole new sophistication to your sentence structures, and it will help you understand some important punctuation rules. This chapter will prepare you for those future lessons.

The Study of Adjectives

A. Adjectives are words that describe nouns and pronouns, which is the same thing as saying that adjectives describe people, places, things, and ideas.

B. Adjectives are easy to use and easy to spot. Can you find the adjective in the following sentence?

She snuck through the halls in red sneakers.

C. Of course *red* pops out as describing the noun *sneakers*. Aren't adjectives easy?

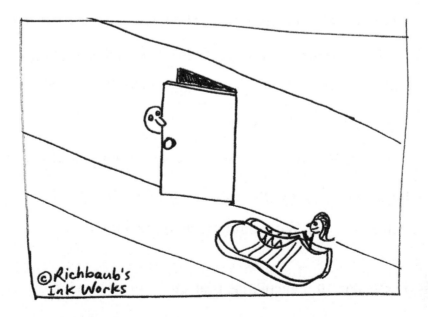

©Richbaub's Ink Works

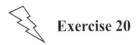 **Exercise 20**

Part 1: Write adjective-noun pairs—come up with a noun and put an adjective before it.

1. _____

2. _____

3. _____

4. _____

5. _____

Part 2: Write prepositional phrases that have adjectives describing the o.p.'s (objects of the preposition).

6. _____

7. _____

8. _____

PREPS for You!
(you're welcome)
about
above
across
after
against
along
around
at
before
behind
below
beneath
beside
between
beyond
by
down
during
for
from
in
in front of
inside
instead of
into
near
next to
of
off
on
out
over
through
to
toward
under
until
up
with
without

Quick Fact: The most common adjectives in the world are the "Articles." The Articles are *a*, *an*, and *the*.

Here's a sentence that, technically, includes three adjectives:

The chef cut an orange with a knife.

For our purposes, though, when hunting for Adjectives, we will ignore Articles; there are just too many of them!!

The Locations of Adjectives

A. Most adjectives are found just before a noun, like in the adjective-noun pairs in the previous exercise. Here's another example:

The warm sunshine spread across the lawn.

Above, *warm* is an adjective describing the noun *sunshine*.

B. However, adjectives can also be found reaching back over linking verbs to describe the subject of a sentence. Here are some examples:

1. Everyone was cold.

Above, *cold* is an adjective describing *everyone*, the subject of the sentence.

2. The children on the swings seemed happy.

Above, *happy* is an adjective describing *children*, the subject of the sentence.

C. Adjectives after linking verbs—the adjectives that reach back to describe subjects—are called **Predicate Adjectives.**

1. "Regular" Adjective: The <u>tall</u> building rose into the clouds.

2. Predicate Adjective: Your grade on the test was <u>excellent</u>!

Exercise 21

Part 1: Write prepositional phrases that have regular adjectives describing the o.p.'s (objects of the preposition).

1. _____

2. _____

3. _____

In Part 2 you will need to use linking verbs:

> **"Classic" Linking Verb Refresher Box**
> Any form of the verb "to be": **am, are, is, was, were, be, been, being**
>
> Any form of the verb "to seem": **seem, seems, seemed**
>
> Any form of the verb "to become": **become, becomes, became, becoming**

Part 2: *Sentence Puzzles* ✠╫✠ Carefully follow the directions for each sentence, and be sure to use a DIFFERENT VERB in each.

4. Write a sentence that has a prepositional phrase and a Predicate Adjective. (Remember, in order to have a Predicate Adjective your verb must be a linking verb.)

_____

_____

5. Write a sentence that has a pronoun for a subject (see p. 25, 30-31), a Predicate Adjective, and two prepositional phrases. (Remember, in order to have a Predicate Adjective your verb must be a linking verb.)

_____

_____

6. Write a sentence that has two personal pronouns for subjects (see p. 84), one verb, and a Predicate Adjective. (Remember, in order to have a Predicate Adjective your verb must be a linking verb.)

_____

_____

7. Write a sentence that includes two regular adjectives, begins with a prepositional phrase, and has a "polluted" verb phrase. (See p. 109 for common polluting words.)

_____

_____

PREPS for You! *(you're welcome)*

about
above
across
after
against
along
around
at
before
behind
below
beneath
beside
between
beyond
by
down
during
for
from
in
in front of
inside
instead of
into
near
next to
of
off
on
out
over
through
to
toward
under
until
up
with
without

Extra Practice with Adjectives

<u>Directions</u>: Draw a single underline beneath regular adjectives and a double underline beneath predicate adjectives in the following sentences. Each sentence has at least one adjective.

**Be sure to mark prepositional phrases, verbs, and subjects BEFORE you make your final decisions about adjectives!

1. The lighted bridge over the river looks magnificent at night.

2. The winning catch in the championship game was made by Peter.

3. On Monday my mom may still take me to the mall.

4. By the way, Peyton and I do not enjoy scary movies.

5. The new crossing guard near our bus stop seems really unfriendly.

6. Zain and he should arrive at the downtown airport before noon.

7. This soup tastes delicious!

8. That is terrible!

9. Between Dion and him sat a tiny mouse.

10. Could you lend me your lucky eraser for the math test?

Predicate Adjectives vs. Predicate Nominatives

A. Predicate Adjectives have a close cousin called Predicate Nominatives.

B. A Predicate Nominative, like a Predicate Adjective, is found after a linking verb, and it reaches back over the verb to describe the subject.

C. However, Predicate Nominatives are not actually adjectives; they are nouns and pronouns that, technically, *rename* the subject–which is another way to describe the subject.

D. Take a look at some examples. The underlined words are Predicate Nominatives:

My father was a <u>fireman</u>.

The centerpiece at the wedding will be a carved ice <u>statue</u>.

He becomes an absolute <u>maniac</u> on the football field.

Have you ever been an <u>actor</u> in a play?

E. In each sentence above, the underlined word reaches back over a linking verb to describe (rename) the subject. Also, each descriptive word is actually a noun, so they are called Predicate Nominatives instead of Predicate Adjectives. (Predicate Adjectives are always adjectives.)

F. Here are some more examples of the similarities and differences between Predicate Adjectives and Predicate Nominatives:

This coffee is hot. (*Hot* describes the subject, coffee, and since the word *hot* is an adjective, it is a Predicate *Adjective*.)

After six weeks the larvae became a butterfly. (*Butterfly* describes/renames the subject, larvae, and since the word *butterfly* is a noun, it is a Predicate *Nominative*.)

G. Keep in mind that not all linking verb sentences have Predicate Adjectives or Predicate Nominatives:

I have never been on a roller coaster.

The girls were at their lockers before class.

A Trick for Finding Predicate Adjectives & Predicate Nominatives

A. If you're looking at a sentence that has a linking verb, and you're wondering how to locate the Predicate Adjective or Predicate Nominative, there is a little trick you can use.

B. Make a question using this formula: "S + V + who or what?"

Example:

The children became cold at the ballgame.

Take your subject, children, and your verb, became, and ask, "Who or what?"

"Children became who or what?"

C. The answer, cold, is your Predicate Adjective or Predicate Nominative—now decide if you've found a descriptive word (adjective) or a person, place, thing, or idea (noun or pronoun).

D. A descriptive word would be a Predicate Adjective, while a person, place, thing, or idea would be a Predicate Nominative.

E. In the example, *cold* is a descriptive word, so it's a Predicate Adjective.

F. Please note: Predicate Nominatives are NEVER found inside prepositional phrases!

Richbaub's Introduction to Middle School Grammar **Third Edition** © 2023 Richbaub's Ink Works *all rights reserved*

Exercise 22

You'll need to use linking verbs in this exercise:

```
"Classic" Linking Verb Refresher Box
Any form of the verb "to be": am, are, is, was, were, be, been, being

Any form of the verb "to seem": seem, seems, seemed

Any form of the verb "to become": become, becomes, became, becoming
```

Part 1: Write sentences that have Predicate Nominatives. Remember, only linking verb sentences have Predicate Nominatives. Limit your sentences to 12 words or less, and **use a DIFFERENT VERB for each sentence**.

1. _____

2. **(Use a verb phrase in this sentence.)** _____

_____

Part 2: Write sentences that have Predicate Adjectives. Remember, only linking verb sentences have Predicate Adjectives. Limit your sentences to 12 words or less, and **use a DIFFERENT VERB for each sentence**.

3. _____

4. **(Use a "polluted" verb phrase in this sentence.)** _____

_____

Part 3: In the following linking verb sentences, find and label Predicate Adjectives (PA) and Predicate Nominatives (PN).

Common Polluting Words
not
never
still
already
almost
also
-ly words

5. The glacier will gradually become smaller.

6. The social studies teacher seems quite nice.

7. That party was a little too crazy for me!

8. My opponent is a great warrior.

Part 4: Write prepositional phrases that have regular adjectives describing the o.p.'s (objects of the prepositions).

9. _____

10. _____

Predicate Nominatives & Personal Pronouns

A. Guess what? Remember those annoying little personal pronouns? Well, they're back!

B. When you use a personal pronoun as a Predicate Nominative, you must choose a Nominative Case Personal Pronoun.

Once again, here are all of the personal pronouns:

Objective Case Personal Pronouns	Nominative Case Personal Pronouns
me	I
you	you
her	she
it	it
him	he
us	we
them	they
whom	who

Use for Predicate Nominatives …Get it? *Nominative* Case for Predicate *Nominatives.* Pretty clever, huh?

As you can see, *you* and *it* are both objective <u>and</u> nominative case personal pronouns. They are "all-purpose" personal pronouns that can be used anywhere.

C. Here are some examples:

I admitted that the thief was I.

For the school play the directors will be she and I. (two predicate nominatives)

D. Yes, the sentences above do sound a bit funny to the untrained ear. However, you apply this rule all the time in sentences that sound perfectly normal, as in the questions below:

Who is he?   **Who are they?**   **Who was she?**

Each sentence above follows the personal pronoun rule for Predicate Nominatives:

After linking verbs, choose <u>nominative</u> case personal pronouns.

E. Sticking to the rule, the following sentences are also correct, even though they may sound a little odd to your ear:

It is she.

Your guests could be they.

The best runners are she and David.

For this project your partners will be he and she.

The contestant would be Rebecca or I.

Our guides during the trip were she and Mark.

> **Who talks like this??**
>
> *Certainly no one roaming the hallways between classes! But you should realize that the rules of grammar studied in this book pertain to academic writing. In an academic (or professional) setting, expertise with the language is quite rare and highly respected.*

F. Something worth noting here is that our rule for personal pronouns and prepositional phrases hasn't changed! You still must use Objective Case Personal Pronouns inside prepositional phrases:

Those presents are (for me.)

They were (with us) yesterday.

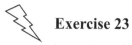 **Exercise 23**

You'll need to use personal pronouns and linking verbs in this exercise:

"Classic" Linking Verb Refresher Box

Any form of the verb "to be": **am, are, is, was, were, be, been, being**

Any form of the verb "to seem": **seem, seems, seemed**

Any form of the verb "to become": **become, becomes, became, becoming**

Objective Case Personal Pronouns	Nominative Case Personal Pronouns
me	I
you	you
her	she
it	it
him	he
us	we
them	they
whom	who

As you can see, *you* and *it* are both objective <u>and</u> nominative case personal pronouns. They are "all-purpose" personal pronouns that can be used anywhere.

Part 1: *Sentence Puzzles* �✚populated   Write sentences as directed.

1. Write a sentence that has a personal pronoun for a Predicate Nominative. Remember to use a linking verb and a nominative case personal pronoun. Limit your sentence to 12 words or less.

_____

_____

2. Write a sentence that has a Predicate Adjective. Remember to use a linking verb. Limit your sentence to 12 words or less. **(Do NOT use the same verb you used in the sentence above!)**

_____

_____

3. Write a sentence that has two Predicate Nominatives where both are personal pronouns. Remember to use a linking verb and nominative case personal pronouns. Limit your sentence to 12 words or less. **(Do NOT repeat any of the verbs used in the sentences above!)**

_____

_____

Part 2: In the following sentences, surround the prepositional phrases with parentheses.
(Ignore the blank lines after each sentence for now—you will use them in Part 7.)

4. The hungry dog grabbed a sandwich from the table. _____

5. During the test Matt seemed confused. _____

6. On the green hill over yonder the cows munch on grass. _____

7. The best artists in the class are he and Jackie. _____

Part 3: Mark the verbs. Use a box for action verbs and an "L" shape for linking verbs.

Part 4: Circle the subjects.

Part 5: Each sentence has either one adjective OR one Predicate Adjective—underline it.

Part 6: Draw an arrow from the Adjective or Predicate Adjective to the word being described.

Part 7: Finally, after each sentence identify the word being described (by the Adjective or Predicate Adjective) as a Subject (S) or Object of the Preposition (OP).

<table>
<tr><td>PREPS for You!
(you're welcome)</td></tr>
<tr><td>about
above
across
after
against
along
around
at
before
behind
below
beneath
beside
between
beyond
by
down
during
for
from
in
in front of
inside
instead of
into
near
next to
of
off
on
out
over
through
to
toward
under
until
up
with
without</td></tr>
</table>

Extra Practice for Evaluation 11

Part 1: In the blank after each sentence, identify the underlined word as either an Adjective (ADJ), Predicate Adjective (PA), or Predicate Nominative (PN).

1. She should have been more <u>careful</u> with her money. _____

2. Rover's barking was a great burglar <u>alarm</u>. _____

3. The person most responsible is <u>she</u>. _____

4. Her statements about the suspect were completely <u>true</u>. _____

5. The car in my uncle's garage is a 1969 <u>Mustang</u>. _____

6. My mom and I looked exhausted after our <u>shopping</u> trip. _____

7. Our representatives are Jake, <u>Tom</u>, and I. _____

Part 2: *Sentence Puzzles* ✚✚✚ Write sentences as directed.

8. Write a sentence that begins with a prepositional phrase and has a Predicate Adjective. Remember to use a linking verb. Limit your sentence to 12 words or less.

_____

_____

9. Write a sentence that has two personal pronoun Predicate Nominatives. Don't forget to use a linking verb. Limit your sentence to 12 words or less–keep it simple!

_____

_____

10. Write a sentence that has an *action verb* verb phrase and three regular adjectives.

_____

_____

Part 3: Write prepositional phrases that have adjectives describing the o.p.'s (objects of the preposition).

11. _____   13. _____

12. _____   14. _____

 Evaluation 11: Adjectives, Predicate Adjectives, & Predicate Nominatives + Pronoun Usage with Predicate Nominatives – Are you ready now?

BTW: There will be both Personal Pronoun & Classic Linking Verbs Refresher Boxes on the test.

Chapter 8

Adverbs

Adverbs are the difficult cousins of adjectives, for although their purpose, like adjectives, is to describe, exactly how or what an adverb describes is not always clear to students. Once you get it, though, your knowledge of adverbs will come in handy when trying to write and speak well.

For instance, deciding when to use well *vs. when to use* good *has to do with knowing about adverbs. In addition, a popular technique you can use to improve your sentence variety is to begin sentences with adverbs once in a while.*

Later, when you become a more advanced writer, you will discover groups of words—phrases and clauses—that also function as adverbs, and certain punctuation and sentence variety concepts are connected to a knowledge of these things...

Study of Adverbs

A. Adverbs are the most difficult part of speech. Like Adjectives, Adverbs are descriptive words, but, unlike Adjectives, Adverbs do **not** describe Nouns and Pronouns.

B. Adverbs describe Verbs, Adjectives, as well as other Adverbs.

C. Adjectives and Adverbs at work:

ADJECTIVES AT WORK

giant ocean

blue fabric

famous actor

ADVERBS AT WORK

incredibly famous

walk quickly

very quietly

The Questions Adverbs Answer

A. The most important thing to know about Adverbs is that whenever they describe something, they answer one of the following questions about whatever it is they're describing:

"When?"   "Where?"   "How?"

B. Practice examples:

1.) **Yesterday we rode our bikes to the park.**

THE ADVERB *yesterday* ANSWERS (circle one)
  A. *when?*
  B. *where?*
  C. *how?*

ABOUT THE WORD *rode*, WHICH IS A(N) (circle one)
  A. *verb*
  B. *adjective*
  C. *adverb*

2.) **The Pearsons will be building a house here in the fall.**

THE ADVERB *here* ANSWERS (circle one)
  A. *when?*
  B. *where?*
  C. *how?*

ABOUT *will be building*, WHICH IS A(N) (circle one)
  A. *verb*
  B. *adjective*
  C. *adverb*

Are you getting the hang of adverbs?

C. More practice examples:

1.) David **gently** rocked the baby.

THE ADVERB *gently* ANSWERS (circle one) *when?   where?   how?*

ABOUT *rocked*, WHICH IS A(N) (circle one) *verb   adjective   adverb*

2.) They will be arriving **very soon.**

(There are two adverbs in this sentence.)

THE ADVERB *soon* ANSWERS (circle one) *when?   where?   how?*

ABOUT *will be arriving*, WHICH IS A(N) (circle one) *verb   adjective   adverb*

IN ADDITION, THE ADVERB *very* ANSWERS (circle one) *when?   where?   how?*

ABOUT *soon*, WHICH IS A(N) (circle one) *verb   adjective   adverb*

You're alwight, Dude.

© Richbaub's Ink Works

Exercise 24

Part 1: Fill in the blank with an adverb that answers the question below the blank.

1. we will eat _____
   (When?)

2. ran _____ around the track
   (How?)

3. were _____ studying for a big test
   (When?)

4. _____ turned left
   (How?)

5. sat _____
   (Where?)

6. _____ bright jacket
   (How?)

Part 2: Locating adjectives

Here's a terrific way to look at the difference between adjectives and adverbs:

> **Adjectives** describe nouns and pronouns (people, places, things, and ideas)
>
> **Adverbs** answer When? Where? and How?

In items 1 through 6 above, there are two adjectives (ignore the articles). Write the adjectives below:

7. _____

8. _____

The Hunt for Adverbs

A. What's most difficult about adverbs is that an adverb's location in a sentence doesn't follow any kind of pattern.

B. For instance, so far we've seen that nouns and pronouns can be **subjects**, **objects of prepositions**, and **predicate nominatives**. Each of these things is found in certain areas of a sentence:

- subjects toward the beginning
- o.p.'s at the end of prepositional phrases
- predicate nominatives after linking verbs

C. So when you are looking for nouns and pronouns, you have an idea where they can be found.

D. The locations of **verbs**, **adjectives**, and **predicate adjectives** are also pretty consistent:

- verbs are predictably found toward the middle of a sentence
- adjectives are typically right next to the words they describe
- predicate adjectives are always after linking verbs

E. **Adverbs aren't so predictable.** Below, look again at the sentences we were working with. The <u>adverbs are all over the place</u>!

> **Yesterday we rode our bikes to the park.**
>
> **The Pearsons will be building a house here in the fall.**
>
> **David gently rocked the baby.**
>
> **They will be arriving very soon.**

F. However, if you have a set routine for analyzing sentences, you will be in good shape!

Getting into "The Routine"

A. So far, we've emphasized the following routine:

> **First,** surround prepositional phrases with parentheses.
> **Second,** mark the verb(s) with a box (action verb) or an "L" shape (linking verb).
> **Third,** circle the subject(s).

On any kind of grammar exercise, you should ALWAYS approach each sentence this way—it will help immensely in your hunt for adjectives and adverbs.

B. Only after completing "The Routine" should you look for your descriptive words, adjectives and adverbs.

C. Let's begin the hunt for adjectives and adverbs by running through an example:

(After the meal) the (children) [sat] quietly (in the family room.)

D. Above, the descriptive words should stand out because you have eliminated some words from consideration:

- Your subject and your verb are obviously not adjectives or adverbs.

- The first and last words of the prepositional phrases are not adjectives or adverbs since the first words are prepositions and the last words are nouns or pronouns.

- Now you can concentrate on just the leftover words to find adjectives and adverbs!

After **the** meal **the** children sat **quietly** in **the family** room.

E. In our example sentence...

Quietly is an **adverb** answering the question "how?" about the verb *sat.*

Family is an **adjective** describing the noun *room.*

(And of course *the* is an article [a type of adjective], but we don't label articles!)

F. Here are some more examples. Be sure to follow **"The Routine"** before looking for adjectives (regular adjectives, not PA's) and adverbs!

1. The fiery coach became extremely upset with his players.

> **First,** surround prepositional phrases with parentheses.
> **Second,** mark the verb(s) with a box (action verb) or an "L" shape (linking verb).
> **Third,** circle the subject(s).

> Adverb: _____

> Adjectives: _____ & _____

This sentence also has a Predicate Adjective (PA): _____

2. Tomorrow your substitute teacher will be Mrs. Page or I.

> **First,** surround prepositional phrases with parentheses.
> **Second,** mark the verb(s) with a box (action verb) or an "L" shape (linking verb).
> **Third,** circle the subject(s).

> Adverb: _____

> Adjectives: _____ & _____

3. I have never asked my teacher for extra help.

> **First,** surround prepositional phrases with parentheses.
> **Second,** mark the verb(s) with a box (action verb) or an "L" shape (linking verb).
> **Third,** circle the subject(s).

> Adverb: _____

> Adjectives: _____ & _____

 Yep, those "polluting" words are ALWAYS adverbs!

Exercise 25

Use "The Routine":

> **First,** surround prepositional phrases with parentheses.
> **Second,** mark the verb(s) with a box (action verb) or an "L" shape (linking verb).
> **Third,** circle the subject(s).
> **Then and only then,** identify adjectives and adverbs.

1. The guy in the red car is driving slowly toward the bakery.

   Adjective(s):

   Adverb(s):

2. Under the porch you can barely see seven little kittens.

   Adjective(s):

   Adverb(s):

3. On sunny weekend afternoons Fido and Rover sit happily on the deck next to the pool.

   Adjective(s):

   Adverb(s):

4. Quietly, he crept through the extremely scary forest.

   Adjective(s):

   Adverb(s):

5. The boy in the blue shorts never runs very fast around the track.

   Adjective(s):

   Adverb(s):

Part 1: What questions do Adverbs answer?

_____ , _____ & _____

Part 2: What kinds of words do Adjectives describe?

_____ & _____

Part 3: What kinds of words do Adverbs describe?

_____ , _____ & _____

Part 4: Analyzing sentences

Use "**The Routine**":

> **First,** surround prepositional phrases with parentheses.
> **Second,** mark the verb(s) with a box (action verb) or an "L" shape (linking verb).
> **Third,** circle the subject(s).
> **Then and only then,** identify adjectives and adverbs—mark ADJ and ADV.

PREPS for You!
(you're welcome)

about
above
across
after
against
along
around
at
before
behind
below
beneath
beside
between
beyond
by
down
during
for
from
in
in front of
inside
instead of
into
near
next to
of
off
on
out
over
through
to
toward
under
until
up
with
without

1. Before the party Tia slept quietly on the couch on the porch.

2. The horse in that barn may gallop through the pasture later.

3. The mother and son have never been shopping at the mall.

4. In the winter, birds look for food under the bright white snow.

5. It was extremely hot at the beach on Saturday afternoon.

6. In the middle of the night fire trucks are always sitting quietly in the firehouses around our town.

7. Everyone on the dock had been in the lake yesterday.

8. That woman should not be walking in the park alone.

(Can you explain why sentence 1 has no comma and sentence 4 does have one?)

 Evaluation 12: The Questions Adverbs Answer + Recognizing Adjectives & Adverbs – Are you ready now?

Some Adverb Clues

A. You may have noticed that a lot of adverbs have the same "-ly" ending. It's true; many "-ly" words are in fact adverbs—**but not all "-ly" words are Adverbs**, so be careful.

B. Remember, if it's an Adverb, it's answering one of the Adverb questions:

When?   Where?   How?

Examples (adverbs in bold print):

After the leisurely walk we were **totally** relaxed. (*How* relaxed were we?)

The friendly man **happily** ate his pizza. (*How* did the man eat his pizza?)

Above, the "-ly" words *leisurely* and *friendly* are adjectives (not adverbs) because they both describe nouns. Adverbs NEVER describe nouns or pronouns.

C. Remember that the words "polluting" verb phrases are adverbs!

Examples:

I will **never** speed in my new sports car! (*When* will you speed? *Never*.)

My friend has **completely** disappointed me. (*How* has your friend disappointed you? *Completely*.)

D. There are also some words that are ALWAYS adverbs. You might refer to these as "classic" adverbs—they are VERY common!

Classic Adverbs	
not	very
never	really
still	too
already	soon
almost	
also	many words ending in **-ly**

E. Finally, if you're having trouble figuring out what part of speech a word is, you're probably looking at an adverb!! This is certainly a lame-sounding strategy, but it just goes to show how difficult adverbs can be.

Exercise 26

Part 1: Surround prepositional phrases with parentheses. A few sentences have no prepositional phrases. (You will use the blank line after each sentence for Part 4 of this practice sheet.)

1. On the bus David handed me a <u>dark</u> green sweatshirt. _____

2. You and Brian will always be my fiercest <u>competitors</u>. _____

3. The captain of the <u>fishing</u> boat gives his orders forcefully. _____

4. My brother keeps his tiny bedroom <u>extremely</u> clean. _____

5. Over the weekend Shantel and Janis studied very <u>hard</u>

   for Monday's quiz and Tuesday's test. _____

6. We became really <u>sleepy</u> during the long bus ride. _____

7. To my dad and me hot dogs at the ballpark taste <u>awesome</u>. _____

8. Bob was <u>still</u> standing in line after three hours of waiting. _____

9. I would <u>not</u> cross a raging river after a huge rain storm. _____

10. That <u>friendly</u> puppy is licking my brother's face. _____

Part 2: In the sentences in Part 1, locate the verbs. Draw a rectangle around action verbs and draw an "L" shape under linking verbs. "X" out adverbs that may be "polluting" verb phrases.

Part 3: In the sentences in Part 1, circle the subjects.

Part 4: In the blank after each sentence in Part 1, identify the underlined word as either an adjective (ADJ), predicate adjective (PA), predicate nominative (PN), or adverb (ADV).

Part 1: In the blank after each sentence, identify the underlined word as either an adjective (ADJ), predicate adjective (PA), predicate nominative (PN), or adverb (ADV).

1. Beside the table Tom read <u>quietly</u> under the lamp light. _____

2. He sleepily fell into a dream about a <u>holiday</u> parade. _____

3. The fountain at the park is <u>full</u> of coins. _____

4. The boys in blue were the <u>winners</u> of the tournament. _____

5. <u>Soon</u> the police arrived on the scene. _____

6. During the winter I become <u>very</u> cranky. _____

Part 2: Complete "The Routine" for each sentence below, AND write ADV over each adverb.

> **First,** surround prepositional phrases with parentheses.
> **Second,** mark the verb(s) with a box (action verb) or an "L" shape (linking verb).
> **Third,** circle the subject(s).
> **Then and only then,** identify adverbs.

7. Mica's very silvery spandex shirt has been sparkling in the sun.

8. He and his small son were already filled with disappointment.

9. In tears, the little girl tugged softly on Mother's dress.

10. From the horizon the sun came up and brightened the room.

11. Bryson had slept soundly in the chair under the lamp.

12. He was also rooting for the little boy.

 Evaluation 13: Finding Adverbs + Recognizing Adjectives, Predicate Adjectives, & Predicate Nominatives in Sentences – Are you ready now?

Chapter 9

Sentence Diagramming

Sentence diagramming requires you to look at sentences like they're little puzzles. Each word is a piece of the puzzle, and each piece goes in a certain place on a special chart that you draw. Figuring out what goes where will help you review everything you've learned so far about grammar in a more graphic way than just circling and underlining things in a sentence.

Sentence diagramming will especially help you get a deeper understanding of adjectives and adverbs and even introduce you to adjective and adverb phrases—whole groups of words that together work as descriptive forces within a sentence.

A. Sentence diagramming is when you draw lines that connect to each other, and on each line you put a different word from a sentence.

B. Here's an example sentence and the diagram of that sentence:

On Sunday Josephine swam in the pool for three hours.

C. Here's another:

Josephine became quite wrinkled.

D. If you're already pretty good at labeling the parts of a sentence, learning to diagram sentences isn't too hard—you just need to learn where the parts fit on a diagram, which is what the next couple of pages are all about. **Do the next two pages along with your teacher.***

*You can also check the answers on p. 169-170.

Richbaub's Introduction to Middle School Grammar Third Edition © 2023 Richbaub's Ink Works *all rights reserved*

How to Diagram Sentences

How to diagram…	Examples:
Subjects and verbs	1. Maria read.
Verb phrases	2. Thomas should have been studying.
Words that "pollute" verb phrases	3. Trains have not arrived.
Compound subjects (more than one subject)	4. Jonas and Ryan are running.
Compound verbs (more than one verb)	5. Emily ate and drank.
Adjectives	6. The tall men are eating.

Predicate adjectives	7. The boys became noisy.
Adverbs	8. The short girls were swimming quickly.
Predicate nominatives	9. That woman is a terrific doctor.
Prepositional phrases	10. Joe went to the game.
	11. The boy down the street is running in circles.
	12. I often run at the park near my house.

Exercise 27

Make a diagram for each of the following sentences.

1. Birds will often sit on the mailbox.

2. Three cows mooed at the moon.

3. Some of the girls may be sleeping.

4. I am very nervous about the championship game!

5. Weeds and rocks clung to the hillside near the brook.

Adjective & Adverb Phrases

A. Yes, prepositional phrases are actually descriptive things. As a matter of fact, many people refer to them simply as Adjective and Adverb Phrases, depending on what they're doing in a sentence.

B. Can you find the Adjective Phrase in the sentence below? (Hint: the prepositional phrase describing a noun or pronoun)

The tent in my backyard is ready for our campout.

Your answer: _____

C. There's also an Adverb Phrase in the sentence above. What is it? (Hint: the prepositional phrase answering When? Where? or How? about a verb, adjective, or adverb)

Your answer: _____

D. Deciding if a prepositional phrase is an Adjective or Adverb Phrase can be trickier than finding plain old adjectives and adverbs. For instance, in the example sentence above, doesn't it kind of seem like "in my backyard" answers the adverb question *Where?*

E. In order to avoid confusion, it helps to know what questions <u>adjectives</u> answer. Every adjective, as well as every Adjective Phrase, answers one of the following questions:

Which one?	…the man *on the skateboard*
What kind?	…the donuts *with jelly filling*
How much?	…an amount *beyond the limit*
How many?	…a crowd *of thousands*

F. Back to the example sentence:

The tent **in my backyard** is ready for our campout.

Do you see which adjective question "in my backyard" answers about the tent? Write the question below:

_____

G. One more thing: Adverb Phrases (unlike regular adverbs) can also answer *Why?*, so adverb phrases answer:

When?   Where?   How?   *or*   Why?

For example:

I am shopping **for my brother's birthday**. (shopping *Why?*)

I run **at night**. (run *When?*)

We have been studying **in the library**. (have been studying *Where?*)

Susan took the quiz **with a black pen**. (took *How?*)

H. Recap:

Adjective Phrases describe nouns and pronouns and answer…	**Adverb** Phrases describe verbs, adjectives, and adverbs and answer…
Which one?	When?
What kind?	Where?
How much?	How?
How many?	Why?

Exercise 28

<u>Directions</u>: In the blank to the right of each sentence, label the underlined prepositional phrase ADV or ADJ. **Hint:** It will be helpful to know what questions adverbs answer and what questions adjectives answer (refer to p. 133).

1. We will be in Michigan <u>on Wednesday</u>. _____

2. The dog <u>on her lap</u> is sleeping soundly. _____

3. A career in medicine is attractive <u>to me</u>. _____

4. The peanut butter is in the cupboard <u>next to the crackers</u>. _____

5. A camel might spit on the man <u>in front of me</u>! _____

6. You should drink some water <u>before the race</u>. _____

7. The joggers <u>on the sidewalk</u> are moving slowly. _____

8. The sweater with stripes <u>in the drawer</u> was made by her. _____

P.S. − How would you diagram an adverb describing an adjective or adverb? Here's how:

A. The tiger ate quite slowly.

B. The very long ride was terrible!

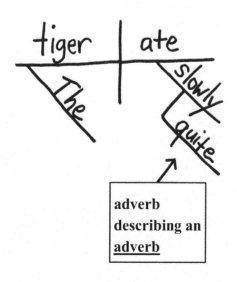

adverb describing an adverb

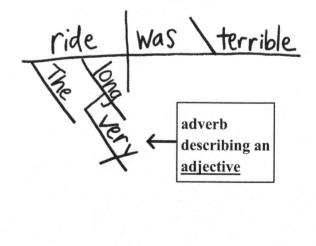

adverb describing an adjective

Richbaub's Introduction to Middle School Grammar Third Edition © 2023 Richbaub's Ink Works *all rights reserved*

Adjective/Adverb Phrases & Sentence Diagramming

A. Sentence diagramming can come in handy when you're trying to tell if a prepositional phrase is an Adjective Phrase or an Adverb Phrase.

B. If you're diagramming a sentence and you put a prepositional phrase under a noun or pronoun, guess what? It must be an Adjective Phrase since it's describing a noun or pronoun.

Example:

The mouse near the trashcan is looking at me.

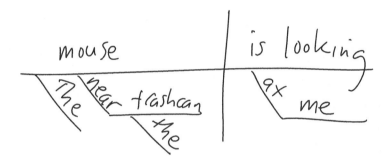

Above, "near the trashcan" is an Adjective Phrase since it's describing the noun *mouse*. Only adjectives describe nouns such as *mouse*! (In case you're wondering, the phrase is answering "Which one?" [Which mouse is looking at me?])

C. And so it follows that if you find a prepositional phrase that goes under a verb, adjective, or adverb, then it must be an Adverb Phrase. In the blank line below, write the Adverb Phrase from the diagram above:

_____

(Which adverb question is this phrase answering?)

Exercise 29

<u>Part 1</u>: Diagram each sentence.

1. The man on the news is serious.

2. The halfbacks and the linebackers are exercising before the game.

3. The walrus at the zoo seems upset with its trainers.

4. She and I will never swim in the pool with her.

<u>Part 2</u>: Answer the following questions about the sentences above.

A. In sentence #1, is "on the news" an adjective or adverb phrase? _____

B. In sentence #2, is "before the game" an adjective or adverb phrase? _____

C. In sentence #3, is "with its trainers" an adjective or adverb phrase? _____

D. In sentence #4, is "with her" an adjective or adverb phrase? _____

Extra Practice for Evaluation 14

Part 1: For each numbered group of words below, surround the prepositional phrase with parentheses. In the blank to the right, identify the prepositional phrase as an adjective phrase (ADJ) or an adverb phrase (ADV).

1. the fan at the game   _____

2. talked about the presidents   _____

3. think of your grandmother   _____

4. has been with the children   _____

5. a car on the highway   _____

Part 2: Diagram each sentence.

6. The new neighborhood beyond the forest is being built now.

7. Our group worked on the Latin project for three hours.

Part 3: Adjective or Adverb Phrase?

A. In sentence #6, is "beyond the forest" an ADJ or ADV phrase?   _____

B. In sentence #7, is "on the Latin project" an ADJ or ADV phrase?   _____

C. In sentence #7, is "for three hours" an ADJ or ADV phrase?   _____

 Evaluation 14: Sentence Diagramming + Adjective Phrases vs. Adverb Phrases – Are you ready now?

The Bottom Line About Placing Prepositional Phrases in a Sentence Diagram

A. The most difficult thing about diagramming sentences is putting prepositional phrases in the right spot. However, there are a few things to remember that can make diagramming prepositional phrases easier.

1. Prepositional phrases at the very beginning of sentences ALWAYS go under the verb. (If you think about this for a moment, you'll realize that ALL prepositional phrases that begin sentences are therefore Adverb Phrases.)

2. <u>Most</u> other prepositional phrases will go under the word right before them. Not all of them will, but most of them will. Have you noticed this pattern?

3. If a prepositional phrase doesn't seem to fit under the word right before it, make a *thoughtful*, *logical* choice. What makes the most sense? What was the author's purpose in placing that prepositional phrase where he or she did? **And don't forget to consider the kinds of words adjective and adverb phrases describe and the questions they answer!**

B. One more important reminder: Words polluting verb phrases ALWAYS go under the verb.

Quick Practice

Diagram each of the following sentences.

1. From my porch I looked across the street at Mr. Maxwell's flowers.

2. The children under the parachute are still giggling.

⚡ **Exercise 30**

<u>Part 1</u>: In the box after each sentence, put an "A" if the sentence's verb is Action or an "L" if the verb is Linking.

<u>Part 2</u>: Diagram each sentence.

1. The wishing well at the castle was built with rocks from a wizard's quarry. ☐

2. For most people the shadows of trees can look really scary on moonlit nights. ☐

3. The boys on that team will usually practice on Saturday afternoons. ☐

4. She and Terrance were always nice to us at the park. ☐

<u>Part 3</u>: Answer the following questions about the sentences above.

A. In sentence #1, is "at the castle" an adjective or adverb phrase? _____

B. In sentence #2, is "for most people" an adjective or adverb phrase? _____

C. In sentence #3, is "on that team" an adjective or adverb phrase? _____

D. In sentence #4, is "to us" an adjective or adverb phrase? _____

Extra Practice for Evaluation 15

<u>Part 1</u>: Diagramming Practice with Pronoun Case Usage Review
Directions: Circle the correct pronoun, then diagram the sentence.

1. The teacher and (she, her) will work
on mathematics after school.

2. To (me, I), the cruise ships in this picture
look huge.

3. (We, us) and (they, them) came to the
picnic late.

4. The men on the stage are Tom and (he,
him).

<u>Part 2</u>: Answer the following questions about the sentences above.

    A. In sentence #1, is "after school" an adjective or adverb phrase?   _____

    B. In sentence #2, is "in this picture" an adjective or adverb phrase?   _____

    C. In sentence #3, is "to the picnic" an adjective or adverb phrase?   _____

    D. In sentence #4, is "on the stage" an adjective or adverb phrase?   _____

 Evaluation 15: Sentence Diagramming – Are you ready now?

Chapter 10

Complements

Wow! You made it to the final chapter! You have one more important concept to learn in order to complete your writer's foundation in grammar. Here we go...

There are three main parts of a sentence: the Subject, the Verb (a.k.a. the Predicate), and the Complement. Everything else in a sentence is, technically, just decorative.

In many parts of this book, we have generally avoided using sentences with Complements, and so please note that while every sentence does have a Subject and a Verb, not all sentences have Complements; however, Complements are very common. Complements come after verbs, and they complete the meaning of the sentence, which is why they're called Complements.

In addition to introducing you to the terms "direct object" and "indirect object," which are terms common to the study of many languages, a study of Complements will also complete your knowledge of the rules about personal pronoun usage (when to use I *vs. when to use* me, *etc.).*

A. You actually already know about two kinds of Complements: **Predicate Adjectives and Predicate Nominatives**--these are the Complements often found in **linking** verb sentences.

B. Action verb sentences can have Complements, too.

C. The Complements in **action** verb sentences are called **Direct Objects and Indirect Objects**.

D. First, let's review Predicate Adjectives and Predicate Nominatives.

Complements in Linking Verb Sentences: Predicate Adjectives & Predicate Nominatives

Review Time!

A. Predicate Adjectives and Predicate Nominatives are found after <u>linking</u> verbs. They reach back over the verbs to describe the subjects. Remember?

B. Predicate Nominatives are nouns and pronouns while Predicate Adjectives are adjectives.

C. Take a look at some examples:

My mother is a nurse. (*Nurse* is a Predicate Nominative.)

The men were angry. (*Angry* is a Predicate Adjective.)

In the carriage the baby seemed really happy. (*Happy* is a Predicate Adjective.)

At eighteen Thomas became the captain of a fishing boat. (*Captain* is a Predicate Nominative.)

D. By the way, Predicate Adjectives and Predicate Nominatives are NEVER found inside prepositional phrases!

E. Some sentences do not have a Complement, so some linking verb sentences will have neither a Predicate Adjective nor a Predicate Nominative.

F. Linking verb sentences without a Predicate Adjective or Predicate Nominative:

Jonathan was in the library after school.

My dad has never been on a roller coaster in his entire life.

Predicate Nominatives & Personal Pronoun Usage

A. Do you remember that there are rules about using personal pronouns as Predicate Nominatives?

B. Once again, here are those moody personal pronouns:

Objective Case Personal Pronouns	Nominative Case Personal Pronouns
me	I
you	you
her	she
it	it
him	he
us	we
them	they
whom	who

As you can see, *you* and *it* are both objective <u>and</u> nominative case personal pronouns. They are "all-purpose" personal pronouns that can be used anywhere.

C. For Predicate Nominatives, you may only use Nominative Case Personal Pronouns. Get it? *Nominative* Case for Predicate *Nominatives*? Pretty clever, huh?

Examples:

This |is **she**.

The spies |could possibly be **she** and **he**.

The winner |is **who**?

The loudest people at the concert |will be **we**.

The players with the most points |are Taylor and **I**.

Who |is **he**?

 **Exercise 31**

Part 1: Complete "The Routine" for each sentence below.

First, surround prepositional phrases with parentheses.
Second, mark the verb(s) with a box (action verb) or an "L" shape (linking verb).
Third, circle the subject(s).

1. The puppy in the park seems totally lost.

2. I have been in the library for two hours.

3. This soup in my lunchbox tastes really terrible.

4. You should not be on the field during the game.

5. On Halloween I became frightened at the spooky house on Elm Street.

6. A fire truck was racing through the traffic at rush hour.

7. The players next to me were Brian and he.

8. In the 1950's and 1960's Willie Mays was a terrific baseball player for the Giants.

9. To Bob and me the picture on that wall looks crooked.

Part 2: In the sentences above, over each complement, write PN (Predicate Nominative) or PA (Predicate Adjective). Some sentences will **not** have a complement.

Part 3: Circle the correct personal pronouns.

10. The player with the most home runs is (he, him).

11. In the front will be Taya, Kira, and (her, she).

12. To Tom and (me, I) the counselors at camp have been awesome.

PREPS for You! (you're welcome)
about
above
across
after
against
along
around
at
before
behind
below
beneath
beside
between
beyond
by
down
during
for
from
in
in front of
inside
instead of
into
near
next to
of
off
on
out
over
through
to
toward
under
until
up
with
without

Exercise 32

<u>Part 1</u>: Choose the correct personal pronoun and make a diagram for each of the following sentences.

1. The winners of the race were she and (I , me).

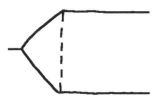

HINT: Use this shape when you have two of something.

2. The gifts from Joe and (I , me) have been placed under the tree.

3. Joseph and (them , they) were cooking on a propane grill.

4. Mary and (he , him) are always studying for English tests.

<u>Part 2</u>: Answer the following questions about the sentences above.

A. In sentence #1, is "of the race" an ADJ or ADV phrase?   _____

B. In sentence #2, is "under the tree" an ADJ or ADV phrase?   _____

C. In sentence #3, is "on a propane grill" an ADJ or ADV phrase?   _____

D. In sentence #4, is "for English tests" an ADJ or ADV phrase?   _____

Complements in Action Verb Sentences: Direct Objects & Indirect Objects

A. Just like Linking Verb sentences, Action Verb sentences can also have complements. Complements in Action Verb sentences are called **Direct Objects** and **Indirect Objects**.

B. Direct and Indirect Objects (DO's and IO's) have some similarities with the other complements, Predicate Adjectives and Predicate Nominatives (PA's and PN's):

1. They also are NEVER found inside prepositional phrases.

2. They also typically come after the verb.

C. ALL of these things (DO's, IO's, PA's, and PN's) are complements, but what are the big differences between them?

1. DO's and IO's come after **action verbs**. PA's and PN's come after **linking verbs**.

2. PA's and PN's **describe the subject** of the sentence. DO's and IO's do **NOT** describe the subject of the sentence.

D. Look at the following complements (in bold print) in action. Notice the similarities and differences between the various kinds of complements:

ALL complements come after the verb & are never in prep. phrases	
1. He has been an **engineer** (for sixteen years).	PA's and PN's come after LV's & describe the subject of the sentence
2. Mary is quite **nervous** (about the math exam).	
3. (Before dessert) you must eat your **vegetables**.	DO's and IO's come after AV's & do **not** describe the subject of the sentence
4. My dad told **us** a really boring **story** (at bedtime)!	

E. Direct and Indirect Objects are both **always** Nouns or Pronouns. In English, all objects are nouns and pronouns, from objects of prepositions, to objective case personal pronouns, to direct and indirect objects.

F. Direct Objects are FAR more common than Indirect Objects, and so our discussion of complements in action verb sentences will begin with Direct Objects.

P.S. — **Stay fresh with your sentence diagramming by diagramming the sentence below:**

In the fish tank near my bed the skittish crab often runs under a conch shell.

Locating Direct Objects

A. In order to find Direct Objects, there is a little trick you can use. Remember, though, to **only look for Direct Objects if the sentence has an <u>action</u> verb!** Here's the trick:

Plug the sentence's subject & verb into this question:

"_____ _____ who or what?"
       subject   *verb*

B. **Does this look familiar?** It's the same trick you can use to find Predicate Adjectives and Predicate Nominatives (see p. 108). Compare the following sentences. The first has a PA, the second a DO:

   1. With her friends Mary seemed comfortable.

      "Mary seemed who or what?" complement = _____(PA)

   2. I washed the dishes after dinner.

      "I washed who or what?" complement = _____(DO)

C. Remember, though—**Predicate Adjectives and Predicate Nominatives are only in <u>linking</u> verb sentences while Direct Objects are only found in <u>action</u> verb sentences.**

D. Another Direct Object example:

The policemen washed their cars on Saturday.

Take your subject, policemen, and your verb, washed, and ask, "Who or what?"

      "Policemen washed who or what?" complement = _____

Since this is an **action verb sentence**, the answer (*cars*) is a Direct Object!

E. More examples of action verb sentences with Direct Objects:

   1. The miners blasted a large hole in the wall of the tunnel.

      In the sentence above, _____ is a Direct Object.

   2. The puppy in the window chewed a rubber toy.

      In the sentence above, _____ is a Direct Object.

   3. Under the water you can see several species of fish.
     (Remember: Complements are <u>never</u> inside prepositional phrases!)

      In the sentence above, _____ is a Direct Object.

F. Many action verb sentences do not have a Direct Object.

   1. Carl thought about the problem for three hours.

   2. During gym class on Friday we jogged around the track for 15 minutes.

   3. The rain fell quietly on the roof above us.

P.S. — **Stay fresh with your sentence diagramming by diagramming the sentence below:**

   The carnival's dunk tank was its most popular attraction.

 **Exercise 33**

<u>Part 1</u>: Follow "The Routine" for each sentence below.

> **First,** surround prepositional phrases with parentheses.
> **Second,** mark the verb(s) with a box (action verb) or an "L" shape (linking verb).
> **Third,** circle the subject(s).

1. The magician at the high school assembly hypnotized my friend!

2. Before a school dance my dad or mom has always washed my favorite jeans for me.

3. Everyone seemed bothered by the smoke from the campfire.

4. That assignment was given to Sheila and me.

5. The lead actors in our school play will be Thomas and I.

6. In the largest cage at the zoo three lions growled at me and my dad.

7. For Lawrence and me this climb may be an impossible challenge.

8. In the swirling wind the umbrella at my table tumbled wildly across the beach.

<u>Part 2</u>: In the sentences in Part 1, over each complement write DO (Direct Object), PN (Predicate Nominative), or PA (Predicate Adjective). Some sentences will **not** have a complement.

Locating Indirect Objects

A. Action verb sentences can also have Indirect Objects.

B. To look for an Indirect Object, put together a question like so:

Subject + Verb + **Direct Object** + to/for whom, to/for what?

C. Example:

                        DO

(Sheila) gave me a ride (to the mall.)

"Sheila + gave + ride + **to or for whom, to or for what***?"*

Answer: *"Sheila gave a ride to…* **me***."* So *me* is the Indirect Object.

☆ **D. You MUST have a Direct Object in order to have an Indirect Object, so always look for a Direct Object first!**

E. Indirect Objects are pretty rare. It's very common for a sentence to have a DO but no IO.

F. Some more examples:

After dinner my mom brought us a slice of lemon pie.
(Remember: Complements are <u>never</u> inside prepositional phrases!)

    D.O.: _____ I.O.: _____

We built my sister a huge sand castle at the beach on Saturday.

    D.O.: _____ I.O.: _____

That fifth grade teacher taught her students several multiplication rules.

    D.O.: _____ I.O.: _____

G. Recognizing patterns in sentences is helpful in grammar—like how the subject usually comes at the beginning of a sentence, the verb usually is in the middle of a sentence, complements typically come after the verb, and a prepositional phrase will usually describe the word right before it.

Here's one more pattern that's helpful to be aware of:

For DO's and IO's, if you pay attention to patterns (you should!), you'll notice that when there are two nouns (or pronouns) after an action verb, very often the noun (or pronoun) closest to the verb is an Indirect Object and the other one is a Direct Object. Look at the following sentences:

                    IO   **DO**

1. That movie gives me the creeps!

             IO   **DO**

2. We bought him a bag of lollipops for his birthday.

*The only exception to this pattern is when there are **two** direct objects:*

              DO   **DO**

3. The lifeguard saved me and Vanessa from drowning.

H. And remember, some sentences do not have a complement, so there are action verb sentences that have neither a Direct Object nor an Indirect Object.

Action verb sentences without complements:

4. The snake slithered under the rocks in the garden.

5. The man behind the counter was laughing at my little joke.

Exercise 34

Part 1: In the blank on the left, write the letter of the statement in the box that describes the sentence.

_____ 1. The rain is falling on Andy and I.

_____ 2. My dad and he felt a little sad after the game.

_____ 3. The puppies are having a blast!

_____ 4. Ties can sometimes be difficult to tie.

a. Has a polluted verb phrase
b. Includes a single-word linking verb
c. Has a pronoun case error
d. I see a DO in this sentence.

Part 2: Follow "The Routine" for each sentence below.

> **First,** surround prepositional phrases with parentheses.
> **Second,** mark the verb(s) with a box (action verb) or an "L" shape (linking verb).
> **Third,** circle the subject(s).

5. A long train carried me over the Rocky Mountains toward California.

6. Before bed Charlie always sang his sister a lullaby.

7. In honor of your birthday we will be eating lobster and steak for dinner tonight!

8. The cheetah is a very stealthy hunter on the African plains.

9. The chef cooked Wally a wonderful waffle on Saturday morning.

Part 3: In the sentences in Part 2, above each complement write DO (Direct Object), IO (Indirect Object), PN (Predicate Nominative), or PA (Predicate Adjective). It's possible for a sentence to not have a complement.

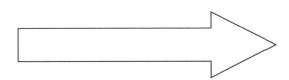

<u>Part 4</u>: Diagram each of the following sentences.

10. The log cabin is being painted by three mountain men.

11. Your cash for the trip may be in that backpack by the door.

<u>Part 5</u>: *Sentence Puzzles* ✣✣✣   Write sentences as directed.

12. Using the verb "did throw," write a sentence that includes an Indirect Object and a Direct Object. Your sentence should be less than 15 words long–keep it simple!

_____

_____

13. In 12 words or less, write a sentence that has a Direct Object but no Indirect Object.

_____

_____

14. Write a sentence that has an action verb but NO complement. Your sentence should be less than 12 words long–keep it simple!

_____

_____

15. Write a sentence that has a Predicate Nominative. Your sentence should be less than 12 words long.

_____

_____

Complements, an AV / LV Sort of Thing

Predicate Adjectives   *Predicate Nominatives*   *Direct Objects*   *Indirect Objects*

It's <u>VITAL</u> to understand that...

DO's and IO's are ONLY found in Action Verb sentences,

and that...

PA's and PN's are ONLY found in Linking Verb sentences! Got it?!!

Your Complements Recap

Predicate Adjectives   *Predicate Nominatives*   *Direct Objects*   *Indirect Objects*

First, identify the verb as action or linking	
Then, make a question: "Subject + Verb + Who or What?"	
in Linking Verb sentences	**in Action Verb sentences**
If the answer is a noun or pronoun, you have a **PN** If the answer is an adjective, you have a **PA**	Your answer is a **DO** **You may also have an IO**
Tips: -Some sentences do not have any complements -Complements are NEVER found inside prepositional phrases -IO's are rare—and you need to have a DO first before you look for an IO	**How to find IO's** Make a question: "S + V + **DO** + to or for whom? to or for what?" Your answer, if you find one, is an **IO**

Richbaub's Introduction to Middle School Grammar **Third Edition**

Exercise 35

Part 1: Follow "The Routine" for each sentence below.

> **First,** surround prepositional phrases with parentheses.
> **Second,** mark the verb(s) with a box (action verb) or an "L" shape (linking verb).
> **Third,** circle the subject(s).

1. The pond in the woods became our hockey rink in January.

2. She asked her a question about the application.

3. The ceremony brought tears to my eyes.

4. Lila and Brielle are in the library.

5. This cool weather feels awesome.

6. The coach threw me three curveballs at practice yesterday.

7. At the park we ran away and hid the Frisbee.

8. The boys will go to the mall after dinner.

9. He is not athletic.

10. In other words, that television show is horrible!

11. Everything in the trunk is terribly heavy.

12. After the overtime game the players seemed listless.

13. Those people are walking briskly.

14. The trees were motionless before the storm.

15. The man brought a cake to the party.

PREPS for You!
(you're welcome)
about
above
across
after
against
along
around
at
before
behind
below
beneath
beside
between
beyond
by
down
during
for
from
in
in front of
inside
instead of
into
near
next to
of
off
on
out
over
through
to
toward
under
until
up
with
without

Part 2: Label the complements in the sentences above (DO, IO, PA, or PN). Some sentences will not have any complements.

Extra Practice for Evaluation 16

Part 1: On the blank line, identify the underlined complement as a DO, IO, PA, or PN.

1. The players on the team were <u>unhappy</u> about the long practice. _____

2. My mother looks really <u>pretty</u> in the picture on the mantel. _____

3. The doctor delivered the <u>baby</u> at one minute after midnight. _____

4. After college my brother became a <u>lawyer</u> at a downtown office. _____

5. The waitress brought <u>us</u> some straws for our sodas. _____

Part 2: Follow "The Routine" for each sentence below.

> **First,** surround prepositional phrases with parentheses.
> **Second,** mark the verb(s) with a box (action verb) or an "L" shape (linking verb).
> **Third,** circle the subject(s).

6. By Saturday Taryn seemed really excited about the big game.

7. The children became cold at the ballgame.

8. The Cavanaughs usually will eat dinner before sunset.

9. On a warm Sunday she and I ate popsicles on a blanket in the park.

10. Grandma will tell me that story tomorrow.

11. Some of the people at the beach are sitting under umbrellas.

12. The stars in the nighttime sky became very bright after midnight.

13. This cake tastes extremely good with a glass of cold milk.

Part 3: Label the complements in the sentences above (DO, IO, PA, or PN). Some sentences will not have any complements.

 Evaluation 16: Complements – Are you ready now?

Objects & Personal Pronoun Usage

A. We've mentioned personal pronouns quite a bit. Do you remember them? If not, here they are once again:

Objective Case Personal Pronouns	Nominative Case Personal Pronouns
me	I
you	you
her	she
it	it
him	he
us	we
them	they
whom	who

As you can see, *you* and *it* are both objective <u>and</u> nominative case personal pronouns. They are "all-purpose" personal pronouns that can be used anywhere.

B. Hopefully you recall that when using personal pronouns for Objects of Prepositions (o.p.'s), you must use only Objective Case Personal Pronouns.

C. Examples:

           op   **op**
<u>For my sister and **me**</u>, Disney World is the most incredible place on earth.

       op
<u>To **whom**</u> did you give your pencil?

                 op   **op**
The ball sailed right <u>over Sally and **him**</u>, and the game was lost.

D. In fact, *all* objects in English follow this personal pronoun usage rule.

E. So for Direct and Indirect Objects, as far as personal pronouns go, you must also only use Objective Case Personal Pronouns.

F. Examples:

                       IO   **IO**   **DO**
My grandmother bought my brother and **me** new bicycles yesterday.

              DO
The bus will take **us** to the beach after school.

         IO   **IO** **DO**
We baked **her** and **him** a cake on Sunday afternoon.

G. And of course you recall that personal pronouns used as Subjects and Predicate Nominatives must be Nominative Case Personal Pronouns.

H. Examples:

My (uncle) and (he) have been hammering away on the dock.

                                           PN   **PN**
The ones responsible for the damage were **she** and Tracey.

(You) and (they) will play for the championship on Saturday night.

I. Here's a recap:

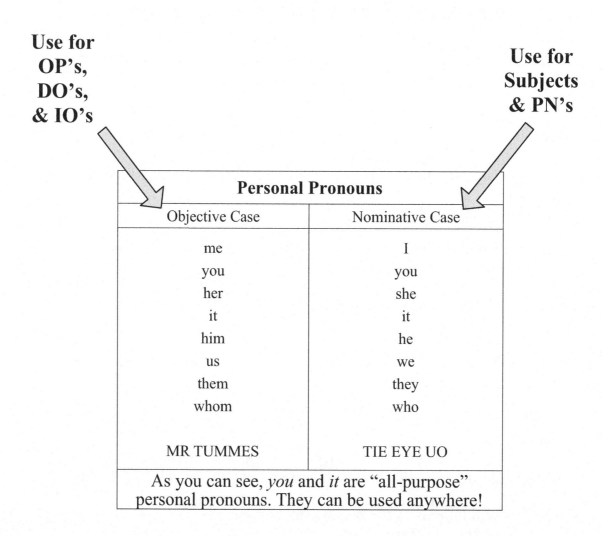

Use for OP's, DO's, & IO's

Use for Subjects & PN's

Personal Pronouns	
Objective Case	Nominative Case
me	I
you	you
her	she
it	it
him	he
us	we
them	they
whom	who
MR TUMMES	TIE EYE UO

As you can see, *you* and *it* are "all-purpose" personal pronouns. They can be used anywhere!

Exercise 36

<u>Part 1</u>: Circle the correct personal pronouns.

1. Under the table I gave (her, she) and my brother some of my asparagus.

2. (Her, She) slid the board into the steel blade of the table saw.

3. Tonight's starting pitcher might be Jason or (I, me).

4. (I, Me) and Billy should have some cash left after the movie.

5. The teacher collected the books from Sienna and (me, I).

6. The boys and (we, us) sanded the corners of the shelf.

7. To (who, whom) do you want me to throw the ball?

8. The counselors were discussing bullying with (they, them).

9. My mom and dad should be bringing (her, she) to the game later.

10. That bike crash wounded (he, him) very seriously.

<u>Part 2</u>: Fill in the blanks with personal pronouns. Avoid using *you* or *it*—that would be too easy!

11. _____ and my dad rode in a hot air balloon in Africa.

12. My teacher assigned Liz and _____ big roles in the school play.

13. The culprit in the bank scandal was _____ .

14. Bring the donuts to Ahmed and _____ .

15. For example, between my mom and _____ there are no secrets.

Diagramming Sentences That Have Direct & Indirect Objects

A. On a sentence diagram, Direct Objects go right after the verb. Put a vertical line between the Verb and the Direct Object. (Don't use a diagonal line—that's only for PA's and PN's!!)

Example:

Jill bought a lollipop.

B. On a sentence diagram, Indirect Objects go under the verb. The line they go on is shaped like the line used for prepositional phrases, but nothing is written on the diagonal line.

Example:

Melinda sold me a house.

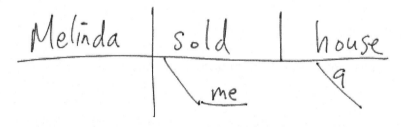

Practice:

Gary gave us a cheese pizza.

Exercise 37

Directions: Circle the correct personal pronouns, and then diagram each sentence. DO's, IO's, PA's, and PN's are in some of the sentences but not all of them.

1. For Jim and (I , me) the test was really easy.

2. Everyone is with (he , him) on the bus.

3. (She , Her) and Aunt Mildred picked flowers for Grandma in the afternoon.

4. At the goal line the quarterback tossed (I , me) the football.

5. The people in the audience will be (we , us) and the kids from the beach.

6. The Tigers had you and (me , I) in the backfield on Saturday.

Part 1: Circle the correct answer.

1. Personal pronouns in prepositional phrases are always in the (**objective ,** **nominative**) case.

2. Before a verb, *outside of prepositional phrases* choose a/an (**objective ,** **nominative**) case personal pronoun.

3. After linking verbs, *outside of prepositional phrases* choose a/an (**objective , nominative**) case personal pronoun.

4. After an action verb, always choose a/an (**objective , nominative**) case personal pronoun.

Part 2: Circle the correct pronoun.

5. The iced tea without sugar was for Mark and (I, me).

6. The wind blew Diana and (they, them) across the parking lot.

7. With (who, whom) will you be speaking at the bank today?

8. (Me, I) and Sheila just finished a bag of pistachios!

9. (He, him) and his dog frequently walk in the park by my house.

10. Several of the boys helped (we, us) with our chores.

11. The author of that poem is (he, him).

12. Across the hockey rink Johnny slid (me, I) the puck, and I scored!

13. Against all odds, Margo and (we, us) reached the summit of Mt. Fuji.

14. The emperor sat beside my best friend and (I, me)!

Part 3: There are **eight** complements in the sentences above. Label each one.

PREPS
for You!
(you're welcome)

about
above
across
after
against
along
around
at
before
behind
below
beneath
beside
between
beyond
by
down
during
for
from
in
in front of
inside
instead of
into
near
next to
of
off
on
out
over
through
to
toward
under
until
up
with
without

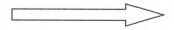

Part 4: *Sentence Puzzles* ✚✚✚ Write sentences as directed.

15. Begin with a prepositional phrase, and include two **personal pronoun** PN's.

_____

_____

16. Use two prepositional phrases and a PA.

_____

_____

17. Use two prepositional phrases, an IO, and a DO. Use "may give" as your verb. Please remember that DO's and IO's are NEVER inside prepositional phrases!

_____

_____

Part 5: Diagram the following sentences.

18. Yesterday Joey and Josh presented the winners huge golden trophies.

19. The bird in this tree chirps loudly at sunrise.

 Evaluation 17: Complements & Personal Pronoun Usage – Are you ready now?

(The sentence diagramming on this evaluation will be for bonus points only!)

Reference

40 Prepositions in Verse

Learn the <u>prepositions</u> in context by memorizing this story!

Verse 1	Verse 2	Verse 3
<u>About</u> the Old Spooky House <u>by</u> My Home I walked <u>Into</u> the old spooky house <u>Across</u> the street, and <u>Behind</u> me The heavy door slammed shut! <u>Above</u> me A single light bulb flickered; <u>Below</u> me The floor boards creaked. <u>To</u> my left, A black umbrella hung <u>From</u> an elephant's ivory tusk. <u>To</u> my right, <u>On</u> the floor Lay an orange tiger's skin. I walked <u>Toward</u> the staircase, <u>Around</u> a large green vase, <u>Between</u> two fat white columns, And <u>up</u> the stairs I went.	**<u>During</u> My Hike and <u>After</u> My Ascent** <u>Along</u> the railing I slid my hand, and <u>Under</u> my feet I felt bugs crunch <u>Through</u> the window The moonlight shone <u>Over</u> the landing <u>In</u> a soft white beam. <u>At</u> the top <u>Of</u> the stairs, <u>In front of</u> me Stood a female ghost; <u>Beside</u> her Was a chestnut horse Whose tail swatted flies <u>Against</u> the wall. I said, "Hello," but <u>Instead of</u> talking, They started walking. <u>With</u> a tall white candle <u>In</u> the woman's wrinkled hand, <u>Down</u> the long, dark hall We went.	**<u>Inside</u> the Chamber <u>Without</u> a Light** <u>Before</u> an open door We paused; <u>Near</u> me I could feel The ghost woman's breath. <u>On</u> a bed <u>Beyond</u> us Something was rustling <u>Beneath</u> purple sheets. Lightning suddenly struck <u>Next to</u> a giant oak tree, And it lit the room <u>For</u> a moment. <u>Out</u> the window Jumped the horse! <u>Off</u> the nightstand Crashed the lamp! And that's when I saw the skull <u>On</u> a pillow And rats wriggling <u>Around</u> the white bones… <u>Until</u> then, I'd never known What had become <u>Of</u> Mr. Jones!

How to Diagram Sentences A

How to diagram…	Examples:
Subjects and verbs	1. Maria read. Maria | read
Verb phrases	2. Thomas should have been studying. Thomas | should have been studying
Words that "pollute" verb phrases	3. Trains have not arrived. Trains | have arrived /not
Compound subjects (more than one subject)	4. Jonas and Ryan are running. Jonas / and / Ryan > are running
Compound verbs (more than one verb)	5. Emily ate and drank. Emily | < ate / and / drank
Adjectives	6. The tall men are eating. men | are eating /The /tall

How to Diagram Sentences B

Predicate adjectives	7. The boys became noisy.

```
     boys    |    became  \   noisy
  The
```

Adverbs	8. The short girls were swimming quickly.

```
      girls     |   were swimming
  The   short          quickly
```

Predicate nominatives	9. That woman is a terrific doctor.

```
    woman    |     is      \   doctor
  That                        a    terrific
```

Prepositional phrases	10. Joe went to the game.

```
     Joe    |    went
                to
                  game
                    the
```

11. The boy down the street is running in circles.

```
      boy   |    is running
  The  down          in
         street        circles
           the
```

12. I often run at the park near my house.

```
    I      |    run
        often       at
                      park
                    the   near
                             house
                               my
```

Index

A

Active Voice
- defined 70, 75
- vs. passive voice 75

Adjective Complement. *See* Complements, predicate adjectives

Adjectives
- "regular" adjectives vs. predicate adjectives 104
- adjective phrases 132
- articles 103
- defined 102
- diagramming 169
- locating adjectives 104, 119–121
- questions adjectives answer 132–133

Adverbs
- "classic" adverbs 125
- adverb phrases 132
  - questions adverb phrases answer 133
- defined 116
- diagramming 134, 170
- locating adverbs 120–121, 125
- questions adverbs answer 117
- vs. adjectives 119

Articles
- defined 13, 103

C

Capitalization
- rules for dialogue 95–96

Clauses
- independent clause
  - combining in compound sentences 88
  - defined 87

Comma Splice Error 88

Comma Usage
- for introductory prepositional phrases 35–36
- in compound sentences 88
- in dialogue 94, 96

Complements
- direct objects
  - defined 141, 146–147, 155–156
  - diagramming 162
  - locating direct objects 148–149, 152, 155–156
  - personal pronoun usage for direct objects 159–160
- indirect objects
  - defined 141, 146–147, 155–156
  - diagramming 162
  - locating indirect objects 151–152, 155–156
  - personal pronoun usage for indirect objects 159–160
- predicate adjectives
  - defined 104, 141–142, 155–156
  - diagramming 170
  - locating predicate adjectives 108, 155–156
  - vs. "regular" adjectives 104
  - vs. predicate nominatives 107
- predicate nominatives
  - defined 107, 141–142, 155–156
  - diagramming 170
  - locating predicate nominatives 108, 155–156
  - personal pronoun usage for predicate nominatives 110–111, 143, 160
  - vs. predicate adjectives 107

Compound Sentence. *See* Sentence Structure, compound sentences

Conjunctions
- coordinating conjunctions 88
- diagramming 169
- in compound sentences 88
- inside prepositional phrases 18

D

Demonstrative Pronouns 31

Dialogue
- capitalization rules 95
  - in interrupted quotations 96
- paragraph breaks 98
- punctuating 94
  - in interrupted quotations 96
  - use of single quotation marks 93

Direct Objects. *See* Complements, direct objects

I

Indefinite Pronouns 30

Independent Clause. *See* Clauses, independent clause

Indirect Objects. *See* Complements, indirect objects

Infinitives. *See* Verbs, infinitive form (verbal)

Introductory Prepositional Phrase. *See* Prepositions, prepositional phrases, introductory prepositional phrase

Richbaub's Introduction to Middle School Grammar   Third Edition   © 2023 Richbaub's Ink Works   *all rights reserved*

Made in the USA
Monee, IL
11 August 2023

40877413R00096